Online R

Access practical templates of the concepts that you will learn in this book as part of the online resources. These downloadable templates will help you implement your learnings in the real world and give you an in-depth understanding of the concepts. The templates include:

1. Project Charter
2. RACI Chart
3. Stakeholder Engagement Plan Chart
4. Stakeholder Register

To access the templates, follow the steps below:

1. Go to **www.vibrantpublishers.com**
2. Click on the **'Online Resources'** option on the Home Page
3. Login by entering your account details (or create an account if you don't have one)
4. Go to the Self-Learning Management series section and click on the **'Stakeholder Engagement Essentials You Always Wanted To Know'** link and access the templates.

Happy self-learning!

This page is intentionally left blank

SELF-LEARNING MANAGEMENT SERIES

VIBRANT
PUBLISHERS

STAKEHOLDER ENGAGEMENT ESSENTIALS

YOU ALWAYS WANTED TO KNOW

Apply the tenets of project management to successfully engage your stakeholders

MICHELLE BARTONICO, PMP

Stakeholder Engagement Essentials You Always Wanted To Know

First Edition

Paperback ISBN 10: 1-63651-151-1
Paperback ISBN 13: 978-1-63651-151-1

Ebook ISBN 10: 1-63651-152-X
Ebook ISBN 13: 978-1-63651-152-8

Hardback ISBN 10: 1-63651-153-8
Hardback ISBN 13: 978-1-63651-153-5

Library of Congress Control Number: 2022947861

Vibrant Publishers books are available at special quantity discount for sales promotions, or for use in corporate training programs. For more information please write to bulkorders@vibrantpublishers.com

Please email feedback / corrections (technical, grammatical or spelling) to spellerrors@vibrantpublishers.com

To access the complete catalogue of Vibrant Publishers, visit www.vibrantpublishers.com

SELF-LEARNING MANAGEMENT SERIES

TITLE	PAPERBACK* ISBN
ACCOUNTING, FINANCE & ECONOMICS	
COST ACCOUNTING AND MANAGEMENT ESSENTIALS	9781636511030
FINANCIAL ACCOUNTING ESSENTIALS	9781636510972
FINANCIAL MANAGEMENT ESSENTIALS	9781636511009
MACROECONOMICS ESSENTIALS	9781636511818
MICROECONOMICS ESSENTIALS	9781636511153
PERSONAL FINANCE ESSENTIALS	9781636511849

ENTREPRENEURSHIP & STRATEGY

BUSINESS PLAN ESSENTIALS	9781636511214
BUSINESS STRATEGY ESSENTIALS	9781949395778
ENTREPRENEURSHIP ESSENTIALS	9781636511603

GENERAL MANAGEMENT

BUSINESS LAW ESSENTIALS	9781636511702
DECISION MAKING ESSENTIALS	9781636510026
LEADERSHIP ESSENTIALS	9781636510316
PRINCIPLES OF MANAGEMENT ESSENTIALS	9781636511542
TIME MANAGEMENT ESSENTIALS	9781636511665

*Also available in Hardback & Ebook formats

SELF-LEARNING MANAGEMENT SERIES

TITLE	PAPERBACK* ISBN

HUMAN RESOURCE MANAGEMENT

DIVERSITY IN THE WORKPLACE ESSENTIALS	9781636511122
HR ANALYTICS ESSENTIALS	9781636510347
HUMAN RESOURCE MANAGEMENT ESSENTIALS	9781949395839
ORGANIZATIONAL BEHAVIOR ESSENTIALS	9781636510378
ORGANIZATIONAL DEVELOPMENT ESSENTIALS	9781636511481

MARKETING & SALES MANAGEMENT

DIGITAL MARKETING ESSENTIALS	9781949395747
MARKETING MANAGEMENT ESSENTIALS	9781636511788
SALES MANAGEMENT ESSENTIALS	9781636510743
SERVICES MARKETING ESSENTIALS	9781636511733

OPERATIONS & PROJECT MANAGEMENT

AGILE ESSENTIALS	9781636510057
OPERATIONS & SUPPLY CHAIN MANAGEMENT ESSENTIALS	9781949395242
PROJECT MANAGEMENT ESSENTIALS	9781636510712
STAKEHOLDER ENGAGEMENT ESSENTIALS	9781636511511

*Also available in Hardback & Ebook formats

About the Author

Michelle Bartonico is an experienced, solution-driven marketer and project manager with more than a decade of experience in higher education and marketing agencies serving clients in a breadth of industry verticals from healthcare to manufacturing. She is a certified Project Management Professional (PMP), PROSCI Certified Change Practitioner, Six Sigma Yellow Belt, and has completed the Google Project Management Career Certificate program. Michelle also earned a Search Engine Optimization specialization from UC Davis Continuing and Professional Education.

Michelle has built and developed teams throughout her career, served in an executive leadership role, and led enterprise-wide initiatives. In 2013, Michelle joined Trinity University (an institution with a $1.7B endowment) where she held several roles within the organization from marketing strategist to Assistant Vice President for Strategic Communications and Marketing to Senior Strategist and project manager.

During her tenure at Trinity University, Michelle led the strategic marketing planning that resulted in six consecutive years of historic first-year admissions numbers along with academic quality reaching all-time highs. In partnership with the Office of Development, marketing campaigns and strategic initiatives were created and implemented - resulting in historic 10-year highs for alumni giving and fundraising goals. Michelle was a lead strategist and project manager for the preparation of the

University's comprehensive fundraising campaign. Michelle was also a lead project manager and strategist to the executive team that successfully petitioned for Carnegie reclassification - moving Trinity from Regional Liberal Arts to the National Liberal Arts category for U.S. News and World Report rankings. Continuing the unprecedented momentum, Michelle led the effort to create the University's first Enterprise Project Management Office and continues to advise executive leadership in the areas of project management, strategy, and communications.

Achieving historic results, Michelle's team was a Top 3 finalist for the 2018 AMA Higher Education Marketing Team of the Year Award.

Other Contributors

We would like to thank our editor, Dr. John Jagtiani for his contribution to making this book the best version possible. He is an experienced business leader and educator with 30+ years of professional experience. He has expertise in cross-industry project delivery and management, solutions architecture, systems strategy & implementation, sales methodology and enablement, management consulting, development of global consulting organizations, multi-shore / offshore capability build and management, training development and delivery, contract negotiations, and vendor management. Dr. Jagtiani has held several leadership positions in organizations including IBM, PepsiCo, Accenture, Marsh & McLennan, and Oracle. In addition, he has also been involved with several entrepreneurial initiatives. He currently serves as an Assistant Professor and Program Coordinator for the next generation of Business Intelligence and Computer Science programs at Northwestern Community College. He also serves as an adjunct faculty member at the School of Engineering at Fairfield University and the University of Bridgeport. Dr. Jagtiani has also taught graduate-level courses at NYU and the University of New Haven. He holds a BA in Computer Science and Economics, an MBA in Marketing, and a Ph.D. in Technology Management.

This page is intentionally left blank

What experts say about this book!

This book is an excellent introductory textbook for those wanting to know about the importance of stakeholder engagement. The succinctness of the text and the breadth of the content covered offer a unique glimpse to anyone curious about this sub-topic within project management. It would be helpful for undergraduate students, early-career practitioners, and entrepreneurs wanting to break into any customer oriented industry. This is a great addition to the Vibrant's Essentials Series.

– James Meersman, Assistant Professor,
Juniata College

Given the dynamic world in which we live, it is crucial more than ever to identify and cultivate your business community's stakeholders. Michelle accurately reflects this need and establishes proven methods that have helped our community engage with the right stakeholders, at the right time.

– Mark McCullough, M.A. in Teaching,
Interim Director-Middle School, St. Luke's Episcopal School

This book has been written in a very simple and easy-to-understand language and will be of immense help to management students. The examples and case studies included in the book have enriched it immensely. This book's content is organized in such a logical and systematic way, that it can also encourage some of the management institutes to introduce a separate course on 'Stakeholder Engagement' in their management programmes.

– Dr. Surendra Rajpurohit, Associate Professor
Mody University of Science & Technology

What experts say about this book!

Stakeholder Engagement Essentials articulates a people-centric approach that humanizes project management. This book provides engaging activities and discussions that allow the reader to reflect on and effectively digest the material.

**– Stephanie Mendeloff, Executive Director,
CREA Curriculum & Consulting**

Stakeholder Engagement Essentials is a definitive playbook for stakeholder engagement. Michelle leads us through the key processes and provides the tools to effectively execute a project. A clear, concise, and contemporary field guide for all project managers.

**– Bob Scherer, Professor of Management and Dean,
Neidorff School of Business, Trinity University "**

Projects are part of our daily lives, yet we often lack the fundamentals to ensure their success. Engaging stakeholders is the key. By applying the tenets of project management, this book provides case studies, templates, and approaches that equip readers for success.

**– Stephanie Jonkers, CPA Controller,
Fullstream Energy HoldingsPri**

This book is well organized and easy to follow for new project managers. It could serve as a great learning tool and reference guide for career development as it includes class (or personal) activities, case studies, and quizzes to help students learn and master all project management learning objectives.

**– Jessica Chan, Academic Coordinator,
University of Texas, MD Anderson Cancer Centerinci**

Table of Contents

Thank you to Vibrant Publishers for giving me an opportunity to share my voice through this book.

To my husband, sons, and parents, your unwavering support made this book a reality.

Special thanks to Jennifer Dempsey for the encouragement.

– **Michelle Bartonico**

This page is intentionally left blank

Preface

In 2014, Southwest Airlines launched an advertising campaign to articulate how their airline differed from others in the industry. The award-winning campaign used the tagline "Without a heart, it's just a machine."

Since its rollout, the phrase stuck with me. It became the mindset I brought to projects and to teams. Initially, I struggled to find the connection between the phrase and project management. Upon reflection, the beating heart was clear - stakeholders.

Throughout this book, you will see reference to Stakeholder Engagement being the heart of project management. I believe as project managers and team leads, we cannot simply memorize the A Guide to the Project Management Body of Knowledge (*PMBOK® Guide*). Stakeholder Engagement is the fulcrum on which everything turns. It represents the people who actually perform the work, are affected by the outcome(s), and whose buy-in is essential for project success. Yet, strategically engaging stakeholders is the area of project management that is overlooked, underestimated, or mismanaged entirely.

Think about a time you were part of a team and it felt empty. Tasks and stakeholder interactions were transactional, team culture was focused on checking the boxes, and the project purpose had varying interpretations. This is a project machine. Inputs and outputs are developed on time and in the correct order. It is perfect on paper. The Project Charter is drafted, the formal kickoff meeting conducted, a list of stakeholders generated, milestones predetermined, and a project management tool is set up. However, while this is occurring, the undercurrent of stakeholder engagement is neglected. Stakeholder Engagement planning is sometimes skipped or hastened in order to stay on track. Or, a plan is created, but never managed or monitored. Identifying the stakeholders is foundational, but without analysis, an engagement plan, and strategic plan management, the project slowly degrades to become "just a machine." What's more, without paying attention to the heart, the machine will fail.

You may think a single project lives on an island, but each project - and its people - represent the company. Every company has a brand and that brand is the sum of its parts. So, whether your project is small or large in scale, you should bring a human-centric mindset and endeavor to deliver value to stakeholders and to your organization. This is a contribution we can all make to the working world - not only for our own project success but for the long-term health of the organization and its people.

Regardless of whether the project stakeholders are employees, customers, executives, or vendors, they are the secret ingredient. With the tools from this book and a people-first orientation, project success is within your reach.

Introduction to the book

Stakeholder engagement is the lifeblood of project management.

This became explicit when the Project Management Institute's 5th edition of the *PMBOK® Guide* added Stakeholder Management to its list of Knowledge Areas. Then, the *PMBOK® Guide* 7th edition further illustrated the importance of stakeholder engagement by including stakeholders as the first Performance Domain and detailing the well-defined shift to bringing value to stakeholders and driving outcomes rather than focusing on deliverables. The evolution of this once process-oriented Book of Knowledge bodes well for stakeholder management and for project managers who possess soft skills.

Throughout Stakeholder Engagement Essentials You Always Wanted To Know, the term Stakeholder Engagement is used instead of Stakeholder Management to reflect the shift from thinking that stakeholders should be managed. Yes, it's somewhat semantics, but an important evolution in acknowledging that engaged stakeholders are more motivated to contribute, willing to resource, and onboard with the project goal(s).

Whether someone is a team lead, executive, or team member, it's essential to know how to anticipate, monitor, and engage people throughout the life cycle of a project and beyond. In Stakeholder Engagement Essentials, you will explore how to balance the tenets of project management with the complexity of human behavior. This book provides both foundational essentials of Stakeholder Engagement along with practical techniques and tools to successfully navigate projects and your relationship with people in an organization. You can apply what you learn anytime you need to move a project, a conversation, or an initiative forward.

Too often employees are unable to wade through the politics of an organization, manage the triple constraints of a project, or are frustrated by misaligned expectations. Project managers invest their time solely in checking boxes and desperately attempting to adhere to the black and white. As a result, projects fall short and interpersonal relationships are damaged. Why? People can be fickle. We cannot force them into following a linear path. And, despite the headaches it may cause, stakeholders are the heartbeat of the project.

Together, we will address a challenge that nearly every project manager or a team lead will face at some point in their career - identifying, engaging, and winning over the right stakeholders. By the end of Stakeholder Engagement Essentials, you will have a playbook for engaging stakeholders and equipping yourself for project success.

Key learning objectives also include

- understanding of the fundamentals of managing stakeholders

- helpful approaches and strategies to use

- how to build a Stakeholder Engagement plan

- and responding to stakeholder scenarios

Throughout this book, there will be explicit reference to the 7th edition *PMBOK® Guide*, introduced in Fall 2021. However, the content will largely reflect the 6th edition because the information in this edition is more commonly understood and professionals have the deepest knowledge of these details. This book is focused on navigating stakeholder engagement in a professional setting, not serving as a PMP exam study guide.

Who can benefit from the book?

Effective stakeholder engagement requires a mix of project management foundations, discernment, and empathy. In every industry and professional setting around the world, you will engage with stakeholders.

People who will benefit from this book include:

1. Students who are seeking a well-rounded foundation in project management.

2. Professionals - from entry-level to senior management - who are looking to learn methodical approaches to engaging stakeholders or navigating organizational politics.

3. Anyone who needs to lead others toward a goal - whether that is gaining buy-in for a product or service, managing a company project, or knowing who to include in meetings.

This page is intentionally left blank

How to use this book?

This book was written to provide people with practical techniques and tools to successfully navigate projects and professional relationships in any organization. It recognizes the nuanced, human-centric facet of project management and includes a chapter on empathy that is important to embrace.

1. Think of Stakeholder Engagement Essentials as a workbook. Make sure to read and engage with each of the activities for practice. You can revisit these throughout your career as you encounter new situations and stakeholder dynamics.

2. It is ideal to read the chapters in order. However, if you already have a strong foundation in project management, then you can dive into specific chapters - either to gain new knowledge or refresh previous learnings.

3. Approach the book knowing you will need to take the information and apply the methods and tools that work best for your situation and organizational context.

4. Use this book to navigate stakeholder engagement in a professional setting, not as a PMP exam study guide.

This page is intentionally left blank

Chapter 1

Introduction to Stakeholder Engagement

Organizations around the world strive to be more effective and efficient in reaching their goals and vision. Project managers have a critical seat at the table for delivering results and value to any organization. But, not all project managers are successful. To shine, project managers must artfully and strategically engage the right stakeholders at the right time.

According to the Project Management Institute's *PMBOK® Guide*, project management is the application of knowledge, skills, tools, and techniques to project activities to meet project requirements.[1]

A project's destiny, however, is cemented by how well the project manager identifies, analyzes, and engages stakeholders. Thus, while the "mechanics" of project

---

1. Project Management Institute Inc., A Guide to the Project Management Body of Knowledge (*PMBOK® Guide*) – Seventh Edition, 2021. Copyright and all rights served.

management are essential to understand, these must balance with the ability to remain people-centric.

Stakeholder Engagement is of such importance that the Project Management Institute added it as one of the 10 Knowledge Areas in the 5th edition of the *PMBOK® Guide* and then designated Stakeholders as one of the Performance Domains when Knowledge Areas were replaced in the 7th edition of the *PMBOK® Guide*. Though still widely known to professionals as Stakeholder Management, the term Stakeholder Engagement is used in this book to reflect the shift in industry thinking that emphasizes people, principles, and value rather than just deliverables and processes.

PMBOK® Guide is PMI's flagship publication and is a fundamental resource for effective project management in any industry. A Guide to the Project Management Body of Knowledge (*PMBOK® Guide*) – Seventh Edition has been updated to meet today's challenges, better align to how people work today and help you be more proactive, innovative and nimble.

(Source: https://www.pmi.org/pmbok-guide-standards/foundational/pmbok)

Key learning objectives include the readers' understanding of the following:

- What Stakeholder Engagement is (and what it is not)
- Why navigating stakeholders is critical to short and long-term success
- When to begin the Stakeholder Engagement life cycle
- An introductory history of Stakeholder Theory

The investment of time in Stakeholder Engagement is extensive, but it's required to meet existing project goals, deliver business value, and set the stage for long-term success.

The tools and case studies throughout this book will help you gain a deeper understanding of how to establish productive professional relationships with people who are invested or interested in your project.

Before progressing to the next few chapters that outline the steps within Stakeholder Engagement, be sure to have a firm grasp of what Stakeholder Engagement is and what it is not. Let's get started.

1.1 What is Stakeholder Engagement

Stakeholder Engagement is a combination of thoughtful, intentional planning and project management knowledge coupled with a lens toward empathy and building interpersonal relationships. It is the art of engaging people rather than managing them. Contrary to someone feeling "managed," when people are engaged, they are motivated, participatory, and more likely to be a resource. Before discussing stakeholders any further, let's level-set by simplifying a definition from the *PMBOK® Guide*. Stakeholders are any person or organization that is, or believes they are, affected by a given project.

As evident in the above definition, it's apparent that project stakeholders are unavoidable. They are the thread throughout any project – creating feelings of joy and chaos in their wake. This makes the Stakeholder Knowledge Area (or Stakeholder Performance Domain in the 7th edition *PMBOK® Guide*) one of the most dynamic in project management.

When the term Performance Domain is used, someone is subscribing to the latest *PMBOK® Guide* where the Stakeholder Performance Domain describes the artifacts and approaches needed to engage with stakeholders.

Tip

In the *PMBOK® Guide* 7th edition, Project Delivery principles are used instead of Project Management processes to further illustrate the shift to value delivery, outcomes, and stakeholders.

Stakeholders are the thread throughout all phases of a project - so it is vital to have a foundational understanding of what Stakeholder Engagement is (and what it is not).

As you navigate project or organizational stakeholders, you will begin to hear references to terminology, methods, and principles from the 7th edition of *PMBOK® Guide* so, it's important to highlight some of the key differences in this latest edition, as outlined in Table 1.1, to ensure you are able to "speak the language" and lead project teams with shared understanding. In many ways, the 7th edition acknowledges the importance of balancing technical and soft skills with its focus on lean, agile, and customer-centric design along with the shift to value delivery and project outcomes in addition to deliverables. Terminology aside, if you are a project stakeholder, you'll probably want your project manager to share the views of the 7th edition because people, value, and quality outweigh the emphasis on process and "rules."

Table 1.1	Key terminology differences between *PMBOK® Guide* 6th and 7th edition

6th edition	7th edition
• Knowledge Areas	• Performance Domains
• 10 Knowledge Areas have processes and inputs, tools and techniques, and outputs (ITTOs)	• 8 Performance Domains are focused on performance instead of just process. Models, methods, and artifacts are the terms used in place of ITTOs and emphasize project quality and value delivery.
	• Tailoring – This is detailed in the 7th edition to further demonstrate the importance of allowing the project manager to adapt their approach to meet the needs of the team, project, and organizational factors.
• 5 Process Groups: Initiating, Planning, Executing, Monitoring and Controlling, and Closing	• These are still valid ways to think about how a project progresses, but in the 7th edition, we pivot to project delivery principles.
• Closing the project is the final stage because the 6th edition creates a clear distinction between projects and operations.	• A bridge was created between projects and operations to ensure that the handoff to operations continues to deliver value to the stakeholder. Illustrating this are the 12 standards that need to remain at the forefront of the project manager's mind as they bring a project to completion: 1. Stewardship 2. Team 3. Stakeholders 4. Value

5. Holistic Thinking
6. Leadership
7. Tailoring
8. Quality
9. Complexity
10. Opportunities & Threats
11. Adaptability & Resilience
12. Change Management

The emphasis on stakeholders was evident in earlier *PMBOK®️ Guide* editions, but the fundamental shifts were seen in the 7th edition - from process to product-value delivery - codifying the importance of stakeholders, obtaining soft skills, and following steps to set yourself up for optimal outcomes.

With this context in mind, let's look at how Stakeholder Engagement is situated within the most commonly discussed framework.

You will most likely hear that there are five phases of project management (Figure 1.1). Stakeholders are present in each phase - from initiating the project to performing the work to feeling the impact of the project's outcomes. For a comprehensive overview of project management, Kalpesh Ashar's book, Project Management Essentials, explains each phase and indicates where stakeholders are involved.

Figure 1.1　Five Phases of Project Management

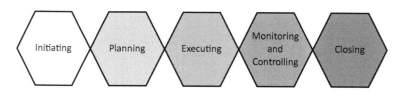

Stakeholders are an undercurrent throughout any project. They are dynamic and ever-changing so it is particularly important to know what the four processes are and where they dock within the five project phases shown in Table 1.2. This is critical so project managers maintain sight of the team's progress in a project.

Table 1.2　Stakeholder Engagement Processes in Each Phase

	Initiation	Planning	Executing	Monitoring and Controlling	Closing
Identify Stakeholders	o				
Plan Stakeholder Engagement		o			
Manage Stakeholder Engagement			o		
Monitor Stakeholder Engagement				o	

Continuing to peel the onion, there are inputs, tools and techniques, and outputs (ITTO) within each of the four processes. Examples of Inputs include the Project Charter, Issue Log, and

Risk Register. Among the Tools and Techniques are, expert judgment, stakeholder and root cause analysis, and interpersonal and team skills. Finally, some Outputs are the Stakeholder Register, Stakeholder Engagement Plan, and updates to the Project Management Plan.

If you're searching for ITTO in the *PMBOK® Guide* 7th edition, you will find it as Models, Methods, and Artifacts where Models include process groups and change management models, e.g., ADKAR®, Methods consist of lessons learned and Wideband Delphi, and Artifacts are documents, e.g., project charters and stakeholder engagement plans.

Tip

In a professional setting, people may refer to Stakeholder Engagement as Stakeholder Management. They are technically interchangeable, but it is highly recommended to think of engaging stakeholders rather than managing them, especially because stakeholders represent all levels of an organization.

That was a lot!

Let's summarize how these phases, processes, and ITTOs relate to one another in Figure 1.2.

Figure 1.2 | **Summary of Project Management phases, Stakeholder processes, and ITTOs.**

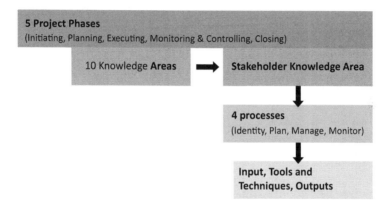

Regardless of the methodology or which edition of the *PMBOK® Guide* the team follows, people can be both the greatest asset and greatest risk. This distinction is navigated by the project manager, sometimes with the guidance of the project sponsor.

A project manager's journey in Stakeholder Engagement formally begins when the Project Charter is created. However, the work of assessing the stakeholder landscape, understanding organizational politics, and nurturing professional relationships starts prior to being assigned the role of project manager. For our purposes, let's assume that Stakeholder Engagement begins the moment the project manager is assigned to a project and is provided a high-level briefing on the project goal.

1.2 Life Cycle Overview

In Stakeholder Engagement, there are four processes the project manager and teams should follow. Thankfully, project managers can refer to the models, methods, and artifacts of project management, e.g., Stakeholder Register, Stakeholder mapping, and Stakeholder Engagement Plan, to guide the project from initiation to close. These touchstone documents help project managers meet expectations, foster open communication, and create transparency throughout the Stakeholder life cycle shown in Figure 1.3.

Figure 1.3   Stakeholder Engagement life cycle

Whether small, large, or enterprise-wide in scale, the Project Initiation Phase is the time to begin identifying stakeholders. In other words, start thinking about stakeholders as early as possible.

Think of the life cycle as a relay race. The success of each step depends on the accuracy and careful handoff from the previous step.

Step 1: Identify Stakeholders – Here, the project manager generates and analyzes a list of people who have an interest in the project outcome. Stakeholder attitudes (positive, negative, neutral) are also assessed. This initial step helps determine stakeholder engagement strategies, clarifies roles, and serves as the building blocks for the Stakeholder Engagement Plan.

Step 2: Create the Stakeholder Engagement Plan (SEP) – Also referred to as the Stakeholder Plan, this is the playbook for how the project manager will engage with stakeholders, communicate, and mitigate issues that could result in a lack of support or buy-in for the project.

Step 3: Manage the Plan – This step refers to the management of the Stakeholder Plan. This step is ongoing because people's behavior is fluid throughout any project. In this step, stakeholders are consulted on whether expectations are being met, their attitudes toward the project are assessed, and the Stakeholder Plan is updated as needed. Keep in mind that the project manager should revisit and adjust the SEP as needed.

Step 4: Monitor the Stakeholder Engagement Plan – Once the Stakeholder Plan is in place, it is at regular intervals that the effectiveness of the plan is reviewed. In the *PMBOK® Guide*, this step is docked in Monitoring and Controlling. This process group signals that it is time for the project manager to be deliberate about logging any issues, adding to a Lessons Learned Register, and noting any adjustments to foundational documents, e.g., Stakeholder Register and Communications Plan.

 Class Discussion

After the project manager creates the Stakeholder Engagement Plan, one team member asks if this plan can be publicly available to all project stakeholders.

What are some pros and cons of this request?

Organizational culture

As a project is initiated, organizational culture is a critical factor to consider. Remember, you are engaging people who have a stake in your project, not managing them. Understanding the organization's culture helps the project manager and project team determine how closely to adhere to the aforementioned life cycle processes and when it is more beneficial to drill into more detail.

A more detailed view of the Project Stakeholder Engagement life cycle is identified in Figure 1.4 using Identify Stakeholders to illustrate the point. The diagram reflects the more micro steps a project manager or project team can take to successfully engage, manage, and monitor stakeholders.

Figure 1.4   **Identify Stakeholders Elements**

Alternatively, when working with teams in different organizations, you may need an even more fleshed-out life cycle that articulates how your team can balance the "by the book" mechanics with the organizational culture. You want this to be specific, actionable, and flexible to allow for continuous improvement. In Chapter 2, you will delve into how and when to address the recommended micro-steps in the Stakeholder life cycle.

1.3 Principles of Stakeholder Engagement

It is often the case that project managers are not in a managerial position or organizational position of authority. Some project managers may have supervisory roles, but project team members are not their direct reports. Despite the lack of organizational hierarchy, they are given the task of navigating organizational power structures, galvanizing stakeholders, and delivering the project on time, on budget, and within scope. This is a tall order - one that is made feasible by thoughtful and strategic stakeholder engagement.

As a project manager, you are acutely aware that stakeholders are diverse, bring different perspectives to discussions, and have varying levels of power and influence. Being true to your commitment to open communication, listening, and acknowledgment of stakeholder concerns should be taken seriously, particularly as you seek a people-centric approach to engaging stakeholders.

1.4 Stakeholder Theory

Since the time "the first humans" searched for food, created tools, and gathered supplies for shelter, there were stakeholders. Of course, more than 2 million years ago, the term "stakeholder" was not in anyone's vocabulary, but the idea that there were groups of people affected by a project and who possessed varying levels of power and interest, was very much a reality. Stakeholder Theory is a mindset. It is a way of thinking that is applied organizationally and at the project level.

It was not until *Strategic Management: A Stakeholder Approach* published in 1984, that "stakeholder" and Stakeholder Theory were formally part of business terminology.[2] Stakeholder Engagement is linked to corporate social responsibility and asks that ethical, societal, and economic impact is contemplated.

Stakeholders have intrinsic value, to an organization and to a project. Thus, relationships with influential stakeholders must be managed and monitored to achieve business goals. They must be accurately identified at the onset of business endeavors even though stakeholders can change during a project for a variety of reasons – a change in scope results in the need for different skill sets, resource reallocation, or the person leaving the company.

Managers should invest in relationships with stakeholders instead of solely focusing on using stakeholders to maximize profits. A relatable term to associate with the Normative perspective is the Golden Rule - treat others how you wish to be treated. Pushing this further, challenge yourself to apply the Platinum Rule - treat others how they wish to be treated. This

---

2. Freeman, R. & Mcvea, John. (2001). A Stakeholder Approach to Strategic Management. SSRN Electronic Journal. 10.2139/ssrn.263511.

Rule is adopted by successful project managers along with the belief that stakeholders offer more value than simply helping to produce business results. Without mentioning the Platinum Rule specifically, the *PMBOK® Guide* 7th edition signals its importance by including Understand and Engage in the six stages of the evolved Stakeholder life cycle. This, of course, implies that project managers see stakeholders as people with many facets rather than either project assets or obstacles.

1.5 What Stakeholder Engagement is Not

When managing projects, project managers often default to what is comfortable - the predictable, and the black and white. These technical aspects of project management can be learned by studying *PMBOK® Guide*. The same is true for learning the techniques and approaches to Stakeholder Engagement with one caveat. Stakeholders are anything but predictable and black and white. This leads us to what Stakeholder Engagement is not. Stakeholder Engagement is not the pursuit of perfection. Success isn't found by strictly adhering to "the book." Why? Because people introduce uncertainty. They behave in ways that are sometimes unanticipated. And, there are team dynamics and organizational politics to contend with. As a project manager, part of the role is to plan for the unexpected. You will begin learning about tools and approaches for this in Chapter 2.

Stakeholder Engagement is not exclusively about shareholders. While a shareholder might be someone with a vested interest in your project, they are exactly that – a person with stake. A shareholder owns a portion of a company and shares of stock are their focus so if they are not interested or impacted by a specific project, they are not a project stakeholder.

Finally, Customer Relationship Management is distinct from Stakeholder Engagement in a few important ways.

- Similar to shareholders, not all customers have a stake in your specific project. Thus, someone might be a customer, but not your stakeholder.

- Stakeholders can make or break a project. Whereas customers, though they provide input, do not typically have the power to stop a project.

- Customer Relationship Management is about sales.

- Building strong customer relationships requires a different process than what is used to engage stakeholders. Figure 1.5 illustrates one that is adapted from the consumer decision-making process. It illustrates the consumer's awareness of a need, the discovery of information through research and advertising, the experience of the product(s) through a trial or test purchase, and any method that helps the consumer gain confidence as they evaluate their options, *decision*, and *post-purchase behavior.*

Figure 1.5   **Customer relationship flow**

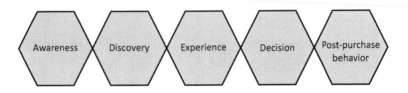

Stakeholder Engagement is not a "one and done" checkbox. project managers should spend the majority of their time focused on stakeholders, as it is an ongoing process. Project failures occur when stakeholders are not engaged, changes and updates are not communicated, and expectations are left unknown and, thus, unmet. The Stakeholder Engagement Plan outlines how, when, and to whom the project team will engage. Beginning any project with the mindset that engaging stakeholders is a core, ever-evolving aspect of the project will set the team up for success.

Quiz

1. The customer relationship flow in this chapter includes how many stages?

   a. 3

   b. 4

   c. 7

   d. 5

2. Which one reflects the correct Stakeholder Engagement Life Cycle?

   a. Identify, Plan, Manage, Monitor

   b. Plan, Identify, Manage, Monitor

   c. Identify, Manage, Monitor

   d. Identify, Plan, Monitor

3. **According to the** *PMBOK® Guide*, **a stakeholder is defined as___**

   a. a group or organization that may affect, be affected by, or perceive itself to be affected by a decision, activity, or outcome of a project.

   b. an individual, group, or organization who may affect, or be affected by, a decision, activity, or outcome of a project.

   c. an individual, group, or organization that may affect, be affected by, or perceive itself to be affected by a decision, activity, or outcome of a project.

   d. None of the above

4. **Stakeholder Management is one of the 10 Knowledge Areas included in the Project Management Body of Knowledge.**

   a. True

   b. False

5. **The "Monitor" step in the Stakeholder Engagement Life Cycle refers to what?**

   a. Monitoring scope

   b. Monitoring stakeholders

   c. Monitoring the Stakeholder Engagement plan

   d. Monitoring the Project Charter

6. **The "Manage" step in the Stakeholder Engagement Life Cycle** ___

   a. follows the "Plan" step and occurs one time during the project.

   b. is ongoing throughout the project.

   c. is part of the Monitoring and Controlling process group.

   d. both "b and c"

7. **A shareholder** ___

   a. owns a portion of the company and shares of stock are their focus.

   b. is a key stakeholder in every project because they own a portion of the company.

   c. is a primary stakeholder in every project because they own a portion of the company.

   d. None of the above

8. **Stakeholder Engagement is NOT** ___

   a. "One and done"

   b. the pursuit of perfection

   c. shareholder management

   d. All of the above

9. **Project failures occur when ____**

   a. stakeholders are not engaged, changes and updates are communicated, and expectations are left unknown and, thus, unmet.

   b. the project charter is outdated, the Executive Sponsor assigns the team, and stakeholders are not engaged early.

   c. stakeholders are not engaged, changes and updates are not communicated, and expectations are left unknown and, thus, unmet.

   d. the project charter is outdated, changes and updates are not communicated, and the Executive Sponsor assigns the team.

10. **In the *PMBOK® Guide* 7th edition, ITTOs were replaced by Models, Methods, and Artifacts.**

    a. True

    b. False

Answers	1 – d	2 – a	3 – c	4 – a	5 – c
	6 – d	7 – a	8 – d	9 – c	10 – a

Chapter Summary

◆ A stakeholder is an individual, group, or organization that may affect, be affected by, or perceive itself to be affected by a decision, activity, or outcome of a given project.

◆ The term Stakeholder Management is still used in the workplace, but Stakeholder Engagement reflects the shift from "managing" stakeholders to "engaging" them.

◆ The *PMBOK® Guide* 7th edition illustrates a significant shift from processes and deliverables to principles and outcomes.

◆ There are five phases to projects (initiation, planning, executing, monitoring and controlling, and closing).

◆ Stakeholder Management is one of the 10 Knowledge Areas in the *PMBOK® Guide*. Within this Knowledge Area, there are four processes and each one has ITTOs.

◆ In the *PMBOK® Guide* 7th edition, Knowledge Areas were replaced by Performance Domains, of which Stakeholder Engagement is designated as the top Performance Domain.

◆ In Stakeholder Engagement, there are four processes the project manager should follow: Identify, Plan, Manage, Monitor.

◆ Stakeholder Engagement is not exclusively about shareholder management, nor is it the same as Customer Relationship Management, though some of the project stakeholders may be shareholders and customers.

Chapter 2

Identify Stakeholders

In Chapter 1, you learned about the four processes in Stakeholder Engagement: Identify, Plan, Manage, and Monitor. In this chapter, we will dive into how and when to identify stakeholders and why "getting it right" in the Project Initiation phase is a harbinger for project success. Common questions project managers ask are:

- Who are my stakeholders?

- What are their expectations?

- What is their level of influence and interest?

- How should they be categorized and prioritized?

- We will cover these questions and more, in this chapter.

Key learning objectives include the reader's understanding of the following:

- When to identify stakeholders

- Steps for identifying stakeholders

- What to consider when identifying stakeholders

- How to create a Stakeholder Register and Power/ Interest Matrix

2.1 Identifying Stakeholders

Accurately identifying and mapping stakeholders can make or break your project. During any project, the risk is highest in the early stages because of the number of assumptions made and risks that are unanticipated. Stakeholders contribute to part of this uncertainty. Thus, identifying stakeholders as early as possible will provide the project manager, and the project team with the building blocks to develop three foundational artifacts: the Project Charter, Stakeholder Register, and Stakeholder Engagement Plan. The Project Charter, drafted when the project is initiated, is a touchstone document that sets the expectations for the subsequent documents. The charter outlines the scope, budget, and milestones of the project. Additionally, the charter provides clarity around the roles and responsibilities of a project sponsor, project manager, and primary stakeholders.

Figure 2.1 Project Charter Example

[date]
Project Charter: [name of project]

Overview

This includes the background information, purpose, and overview of the project at a high level.

Define the Problem

Business Case

The business case describes why this project is important to the organization. Why should the organization support this project?

Problem Statement

The problem statement contains a brief description of the "pain" being experienced by the organization.

Goal Statement

What is the SMART goal of the project? The project goal should be related to the problem you are trying to solve. SMART goals are Specific, Measurable, Achievable, Relevant (to mission/strategy), and Time-Bound.

Scope

Post-project scope, will this project likely need maintenance/operational support? Y N

-

Exclusions

-

Roles and Responsibilities
(RACI: responsible, accountable, consult, inform)

Project Sponsor (person accountable for the project success)	
Project Manager	
Project Stakeholders (People to "consult" or "inform")	
Project Team (People responsible for the project work)	

Project Milestones

These include milestones, phases, and stagegates (where applicable to the project). This section should not include every task. The full task list, resource assignments, and notes should be included in the project management tool, e.g., Asana.

Milestone	Date

Project Budget

Charters need to include a formal budget estimate. At this early stage, if all we can do is a rough order of magnitude estimate, that is ok. We should estimate as best/accurate as we can and then include an explicit contingency of 5%-20% or more, depending on risk factors, and make those explicit, as well. If during the project, the project manager and sponsor determine that a material change in cost has occurred, the charter should be revised and new budget numbers included for the sponsor to approve.

Summary of Constraints, Assumptions, Risks and Dependencies

Constraints	•
Assumptions	•
Risks and Dependencies	•

Approval Signatures

_____
Sponsor/Approving Authority   Date

_____
Project Manager   Date

Identifying stakeholders is Step 1 for a reason. In project management, balancing the triple constraint (time, scope, and budget) and ensuring quality and value delivery is impossible without the buy-in and engagement from your stakeholders. In short, the task to identify stakeholders is where the project manager generates a list of people who have an interest or influence on the project outcome. These individuals can represent any level of the organization - from part-time employees to executives, making stakeholder identification a step that requires intentionality, input, and refinement.

The completion of Step 1 will help the project manager gain support, clarify roles and responsibilities, and facilitate effective stakeholder communication.

There are a few potential scenarios you might encounter when first identifying stakeholders (refer to Figure 2.2).

Figure 2.2   Scenarios for stakeholder identification

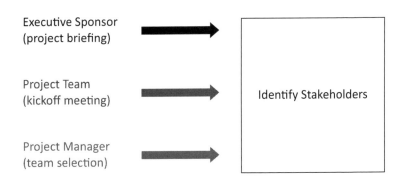

1. In the role of a project manager, the project sponsor (sometimes referred to as Executive Sponsor) schedules a briefing to share the initial vision and business case, key stakeholders, and team members they selected for this project. This is an opportunity to:

    a. List the names, titles, and responsibilities of the stakeholders mentioned.

    b. Ask for insight about their "stake" in the project. For example, how much interest does the project sponsor think the stakeholder will have? Will they bring a positive, negative, or neutral attitude towards the project vision and charter?

    c. Inquire about personalities, relationships, and any additional team dynamics you should know about before the team kickoff meeting.

2. You are the project manager and your team was assembled on your behalf. It is at the kickoff meeting that you begin identifying additional stakeholders and analyzing the interest, power, attitudes, and aptitude of team members.

   a. Remember, team members are stakeholders. These are people who will work closely to move tasks forward and provide the resources to get the project to completion.

   b. In the kickoff meeting where the Project Charter is discussed (and hopefully reaches consensus), additional stakeholders are identified. In this initial conversation, the project manager should capture anyone the group determines that may have interest and influence in the project.

3. You are the project manager and have the responsibility of selecting your team who are some of your primary stakeholders. This is an important task and one that every project manager must maximize if given the opportunity.

   a. Consider the business case and which people can significantly contribute to the "why."

   b. Make a list of the skills needed to complete the project scope.

   c. Create a list of people, departments, or organizations that have (or you can teach) these skills.

   d. Indicate the availability of these resources.

   e. Consult with the project sponsor, if possible, to get buy-in on the list, skillset, and size of the team you are proposing.

These team members are primary stakeholders (internal or external) with a direct interest in the project.

Regardless of the inception of your stakeholder list, the scenarios in Figure 2.2 represent initial stakeholder identification. The compiled list is based on several factors, three of which we will delve into interest, influence, and legitimacy.

If you serve as a Change Manager, or a project manager responsible for helping people through a change, keep in mind CLARC roles. These are critical roles for people managers as they help teams along their change journey. CLARC stands for: [3]

Communicator: This person helps people answer "why, why now, what's in it for me?"

Liaison: This person serves as a feedback loop and proactively engages employees to encourage their input as they experience the change.

Advocate: This person is a champion who demonstrates commitment - with their actions and with what they communicate to employees.

Resistance Manager: This is often the least comfortable role, even for people managers. This role identifies root causes of resistance and helps to provide mitigation strategies to address resistance.

Coach: The role of the coach is instrumental for supporting people's ability to obtain knowledge of how to change and to encourage people to fully demonstrate their acquired skills.

---

3. https://financeandbusiness.ucdavis.edu/obt/services/changemgmt/toolkit/glossary

2.2 Stakeholder Mapping

Now that you know who the stakeholders are, which roles they represent, and their types, it's critical to conduct an analysis that visualizes how to engage with these stakeholders in the Stakeholder Engagement plan. There are several ways to map stakeholders, e.g., the Salience Model, Mendelow's

Matrix, and the Stakeholder Cube. In this chapter, we will cover one of the approaches to stakeholder analysis - Mendelow's Matrix, which categorizes people into quadrants that measure power and interest. Mendelow's Matrix is commonly known as the Power/Interest Matrix, (refer to Figure 2.3). "Power" is used interchangeably with "influence," but be mindful of what influence means versus power, which is usually organizational power.

Once stakeholders are mapped, this data is added to the Stakeholder Register to provide a fuller view of how we think project stakeholders will behave. Remember that people are dynamic and, though Mendelow's Matrix accounts for only two dimensions, it is an efficient way to plot stakeholders in relation to one another. The Stakeholder Register and Power/Interest Matrix provide the project manager with the artifacts needed to draft the Stakeholder Engagement plan.

The project manager can generate this Matrix alongside the project sponsor, or with the project team. The project manager is accountable for successfully engaging stakeholders and, using insight from others, chooses to develop this Matrix by himself/herself. This Matrix can be formal or created on scratch paper. Regardless of the level of formality, this analysis needs to be completed, and the details documented in a Matrix and included in the Stakeholder Register.

Figure 2.3   Interest/Power Matrix

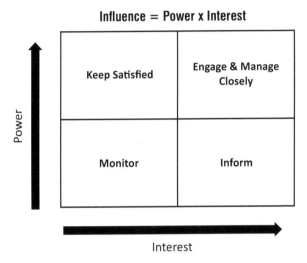

2.3 Stakeholder Register

The Stakeholder Register is one of your first project documents after the Project Charter. In the chapter introduction, you were asked to spot the nuances that make Stakeholder Engagement an art as well as a technical practice. The Register is one of these examples where there are guidelines, but the project manager should use their judgment on which information to capture. With this in mind, we will discuss several options and review templates. When you list stakeholders, consult the project sponsor, the people and departments affected by the project, and anyone else who may be able to provide insight. It's more effective to generate and analyze a longer list. Removing people from the list is easier than being surprised by someone you overlooked.

Step 1: Start at the highest level when identifying stakeholders.

Be mindful that these are examples, and you should tailor these to your project and your industry.

Some examples are

- Employees

- Vendors

- Community members

- Customers

- Lobbyists and politicians

Tip

As you continue filling in the stakeholder pyramid in figure 2.4, it becomes increasingly apparent how to prioritize your communication plan. To assist with this, the Project Manager couples Direct or Indirect with either Primary or Secondary.

Figure 2.4   Stakeholder Pyramid

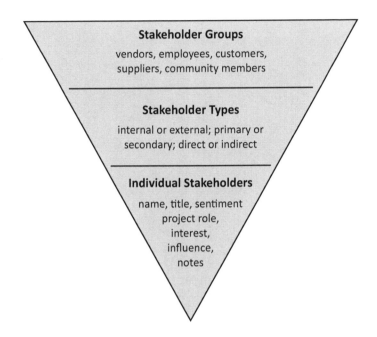

 Class Activity

You are the project manager responsible for identifying stakeholder groups. You work at a university, and your project scope includes the production of printed materials, a community-wide lecture, and a warm message from the university president to the facility.

Write a list of possible stakeholder groups.

Class Activity

You are the project manager responsible for identifying stakeholder groups for a product launch. The proposed product is a toy, aimed at 3 to 5 year-olds, that allows them to learn the foundations of robotics using an iPad or desktop computer.

Write a list of possible stakeholder groups.

Class Activity

You are the project manager responsible for identifying stakeholder groups for a site expansion project. This expansion will be adjacent to your company's main building but in the same complex. The expansion will be used for hospital surgical services and include a dedicated patient waiting area.

Write a list of possible stakeholder groups.

Another way to begin brainstorming the initial stakeholder list is by grouping people as Leaders, Collaborators, or Observers.

- **Leaders:** These are people who you perceive to be highly influential and who are directly involved in the project.

- **Collaborators**: This is a list of people who perform the work in some capacity. Think about the types of stakeholders who "do" the tasks and are a resource in producing a deliverable. These are people the project needs, e.g., suppliers, designers, developers, finance analysts, etc.

- **Observers:** This is a list to be mindful of. This group is composed of people who are not directly involved in the project, have a limited interest, or prefer to watch from afar such as a member of your organization's C-suite. This group of stakeholders can sometimes become more interested as the project develops, and if they have any level of influence, they can become a barrier or an unanticipated advocate. This is a reason to continuously revisit the stakeholder engagement analysis and adjust any mapping, Stakeholder Register, or Stakeholder Engagement plan, as needed.

Tip

Though much work needs to be done in the stakeholder planning process, beginning to categorize stakeholders by their role is beneficial because it starts the project manager on a path to developing a Responsibility Assignment Matrix (RAM). One of the primary reasons projects go "off the rails" is a lack of clarity of roles and responsibilities. Think about it.

Have you ever been part of a project team where there seemed to be several people "in charge" or multiple team members making decisions and you're not clear as to why?

This type of confusion is mitigated by a RACI chart, which shows whether a stakeholder is responsible, accountable, consulted, or informed and in what capacity.

Responsible   This team member does the work to complete the task. Every task needs at least one Responsible party, but it's okay to assign more.

Accountable This person delegates work and is the last one to review the task or deliverable before it's demand complete. On some tasks, the Responsible party may also serve as the Accountable one. Just be sure you only have one Accountable person assigned to each task or deliverable. (Note: It might be your project manager)

Consulted Every deliverable is strengthened by review and consultation from more than one team member. Consulted parties are typically the people who provide input based on either how it will impact their future project work or their domain of expertise on the deliverable itself.

Informed These team members simply need to be kept in the loop on project progress, rather than roped into the details of every deliverable.

Figure 2.5 shows an example of a RACI including dropdown selections. At the top of this RACI, you'll notice a place to link the Project Charter. This is to ensure the Project Charter continues to serve the primary document that includes clarification of key roles, e.g., who the Project Sponsor and project manager are.

Figure 2.5	RACI Chart example

Project Name (link to charter)

Project task or deliverable	Person A		Person B	
Develop Charter	R	▾	R	▾
Select New Software	A	▾	C	▾
Student Journey Mapping	A	▾	C	
		▾	R	
		▾	A	
		▾	C	
		▾	I	

Step 2: Once stakeholder groups are listed, categorize the types of stakeholders.

These are:

- Internal or external

- Primary or secondary

- Direct or indirect

Internal stakeholders are individuals who are within the organization originating the project. A common example of this type of stakeholder is employees.

External stakeholders are those who are interested in your project and are impacted on some level by its outcomes. Examples of external stakeholders are vendors, community organizations, and customers.

Class Assignment

Using your responses to the expansion project class activity, indicate which of these stakeholder groups are internal or external.

 Class Discussion with Solution

There is a contingent of business leaders who previously completed a certification program your company offers. This makes these leaders "alumni" of your organization. Are they internal or external stakeholders?

This is an intentionally tricky practice question so let me share the answer. It depends. The organization should determine its position on this stakeholder group and be consistent so project managers understand how these individuals relate to the organization. For example, alumni from a college may be internal because of their years of engagement and "stake" in the success of the institution, whereas, alumni of a one-time program may be external because their connection with the organization is brief.

Primary stakeholders represent the individuals in the High-Interest quadrant of your matrix. These key stakeholders may have varying levels of influence, but their high interest in the project outcome often makes them a resource for the project tasks. Your project team is an example of primary stakeholders.

Secondary stakeholders are people who have a degree of separation from the day-to-day project operations but are subject matter experts for the project manager and project team. These stakeholders ebb and flow throughout the project, e.g., the General Counsel or accounting office.

Direct stakeholders are intimately involved in or engage with ongoing project activities, e.g., employees.

Indirect stakeholders have an interest in the project outcome but are disassociated with the ongoing operations that get to the finished deliverable. These stakeholders are impacted by the deliverable(s) but react downstream, e.g., customers receiving the printed brochure or commenting on the price of the launched product.

In a real-life situation, the project manager might not have the luxury of spending much time contemplating stakeholder groups and types. That is a reality each project manager must accept and it is their job to quickly evaluate the risk of skipping some of the formalities of stakeholder identification. If the project manager uses the condensed Stakeholder Pyramid, the first step is to list the names of the stakeholders, then the stakeholder type. Essentially, you are working backward with the most specific information first.

At a minimum, however, the project manager needs to:

1. list the names of stakeholders, and

2. indicate whether they are primary or secondary.

The internal and external types are assumed by whether the project manager assigns primary or secondary to each stakeholder's name. In other words, your abridged pyramid would look like figure 2.6.

Figure 2.6 **Abridged Stakeholder Pyramid**

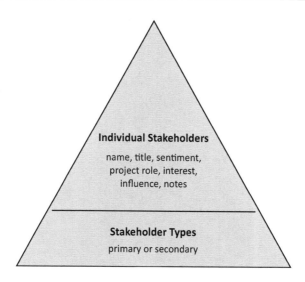

Depending on how familiar you are with the organization, this stakeholder identification process might take you 30 minutes or weeks. Once you have a project team, lean on them to contribute to and finalize the stakeholder details. This document is your Stakeholder Register. Throughout the project, the project manager should re-verify whether the Stakeholder Register is accurate and adjust any changes in stakeholder behavior. This is important because people can change where they are located in the Power/ Interest Matrix and their sentiment toward the project may evolve.

Step 3: Create a Stakeholder Register

Now that you've created your list of stakeholders using the pyramid concept, it's time to fill out the Stakeholder Register by adding what you learned. The more you understand your stakeholders and their perception of the project, the better chance you have of being effective in your stakeholder planning and managing.

As noted earlier in this chapter, the exact information needed depends on the project, project manager, and project team. These especially vary based on project complexity, scope, and impact. Reference examples are available in Table 2.1 and Table 2.2.

Tip

When creating the Register, use Microsoft Excel, Google Sheets, or a tool like Asana or AirTable where you can incorporate dropdowns and multi-select tagging. These resources make the project manager's job of managing and communicating with stakeholders more efficient because they can quickly sort details and update information quickly, as needed.

Table 2.1   Stakeholder Register Example 1

Stakeholder Name	Title	Role on Project	Type (Primary or Secondary)	Interest/ Power (HH, HM, HL, MM, MH, ML, LH, LM, LL)	Sentiment (Positive, Negative, Neutral)	Notes (concerns, priorities, expectations, relationship with stakeholders)
Jan Charter	General Counsel	Legal review, guidance	S	MH	P	Federal regulations, not being consulted

Table 2.2   Stakeholder Register Example 2

Stakeholder Name	Responsibility	Type (Primary or Secondary)	Type (Internal or External)	Interest	Power	Sentiment (Positive, Negative, Neutral)	Location (On-site, remote, hybrid)	Notes (Concerns, expectations, priorities)
Johnny McStakeholder	Web Design	Primary	Internal	••••	••	P	On-site	Web accessibility and overall web best practices

Class Assignment

Brian was assigned as the project manager on a company-wide initiative to expand the East wing of their hospital to increase the square footage of the cafeteria to accommodate the growing demand. His team has cross-functional leaders of various tenure, ranks, and expertise. These stakeholders were employees of the hospital and people who would use the newly expanded facility.

In Table 2.1, list who you think should be on the project team in the Title column and indicate whether they are primary or secondary stakeholders, "P" or "S", in the Type column. Some example project team members are Food and Nutrition representative, financial officer, and hospital patient.

2.4 Ask the Right Questions

The Stakeholder Register is a guide for the project manager and the project team. Therefore, the more information included upfront, the more effective Stakeholder plans can be. It is ideal to develop the Stakeholder Register and conduct the stakeholder analysis (yielding the Power/Interest Matrix) at the onset of the project and revisit this documentation often, particularly at milestones or sprint retrospectives if you are following Agile. However, projects don't always follow how the *PMBOK® Guide* outlines a process - especially about engaging stakeholders. Acknowledging the need for flexibility, the concept of tailoring is explicitly described in *PMBOK® Guide* 7th edition. As a project manager, sometimes it is more feasible to use educated guesswork to complete these stakeholder documents. If that is the case, stakeholder identification and analysis are still worth doing. Do not skip the step of identifying stakeholders and analyzing them in the context of your project. The worst that happens is the documents need to be adjusted as more details or stakeholder behaviors come into focus.

There are more unknowns at the beginning of the project. With this increased level of risk, the project manager must ask engaging questions that yield the insights needed to produce a directional Stakeholder Register and Power/Interest Matrix.

Sample stakeholder questions are:

- What role do you see yourself playing in this project?

- How do you see yourself contributing to the project outcome?

- To what extent are you impacted by the outcome of this project?

- To what extent are you impacted by the day-to-day operations of this project?

- How much availability do you have to commit to this project?

- How important do you think this project is to the organization?

- What level of involvement would you like to have throughout this project?

- Are you the person who can make decisions on behalf of your department, area, or function?

- What level of risk do you consider this project? (high, medium, low)

- How well are you connected to other key stakeholders on this project?

- Where do you think I will encounter opposition? What level of impact do you think this will have on the project's success?

- What are your expectations for the project and project team?

- Do you have a professional relationship with the project sponsor? Is it positive? Negative?

- Have you been part of a similar project? Was the project considered a success?

- Do you have a preferred style of working within a project team, e.g., frequent communication via email, weekly meetings, high-level status updates, use of a project management tool, e.g., Asana?

- What concerns, if any, do you have about the current project scope? Do you perceive the project goal to positively or negatively impact your area?

- How far do they share your organization's values and purpose in this area?

As the project manager, you will also want to be mindful of your professional relationship with the stakeholder and the composition of the team of primary stakeholders being assembled. Oftentimes, the stakeholder you identified is not the sole decision-maker. They represent several opinions and bring those to the project team. This can be a risk, particularly, if you have not identified who these other influencers are. You will need to be mindful of these secondary influencers, how they may impact your primary stakeholder's involvement, and whether the appropriate amount of communication is making its way to these influencers. In the Stakeholder Engagement and Communications Plans, the project manager will include strategies to address stakeholder buy-in, combat unanticipated stakeholder behavior, and convert, or at least, manage stakeholder opposition.

Now that you understand the process of developing a Stakeholder Register and Power/Interest Matrix, let's practice.

Case Study

You are the project manager at Candy Stripe, a community hospital in a growing metropolis. To meet the increased demand for services - ranging from surgical services to radiology to food and nutrition, the hospital is undergoing a 20,000 square feet expansion. You are overseeing this expansion from concept to the grand opening. You have a cross-functional team of individuals, but there is also a wide net of internal and external stakeholders who you and your team need to identify, manage, and engage. Examples of stakeholders include

- **Chief Operating Officer:** John is the hospital's Chief Operating Officer and is the project sponsor for this expansion project. He is highly invested in the project's success, as it will yield increased revenue and align with the hospital's vision to provide state-of-the-art care to the community. John is not involved in day-to-day operations but is available to the project team for visioning, approvals, and consultation.

- **Lead Architect:** Jeff is Candy Stripe's most experienced architect. He has worked alongside nearly every internal stakeholder at the hospital and has designed sixty percent of the hospital facilities. Jeff brings a positive attitude, is detail-oriented, and is aligned with the hospital's vision.

- **Patient Experience Coordinator:** Angeles is new to the hospital, but has worked in healthcare for 30 years. She started her career as a nurse and then transitioned into administration where she oversees the patient experience. While not involved in each project activity, she is a critical subject matter expert who brings the patient perspective to the team. Angeles is skeptical of this project until she sees the schematics.

- **Director of Facilities:** Jeremy has a rocky relationship with Jeff, the lead architect. In a past project, Jeremy's team was not consulted about the construction plan and this led to concrete being poured over main water lines. Despite Jeff's many successes, Jeremy's negative experience created mistrust that he brings to this project. Jeremy speaks on behalf of several hundred facilities employees. He also needs to cascade updates that involve facility team resources. Jeremy is indifferent about the project goal and solely interested in ensuring the project doesn't create unnecessary maintenance work for his team down the road. The project manager will need to pay close attention to the communication between Jeff and Jeremy.

- **Physician:** Moses is a surgeon five years out of medical school. He is chair of the community medical board and quickly became well-known for his work in the region. Moses would use the new facilities daily. He doesn't have time to attend every team meeting, but requested monthly status updates. Moses also wants to be a decision-maker regarding amenities and architectural renderings.

- **Vice President of Finance:** Jisha and John are part of the executive leadership team at Candy Stripe. They have a strong relationship and share the same vision. Jisha has the final approval on budget decisions that are outside of the designated project allocation. Funding is earmarked for this expansion project so Jisha will also be involved in the budget if itis nearing overages.

- **Community Relations Manager:** Joannah has several roles in this project ranging from internal communication to stakeholders to public relations as visible construction milestones are achieved. She needs to receive an overarching project plan with key dates and milestones. And, Joannah should be notified of any timeline changes, photography opportunities, and reputational issues related to the project. She is not involved in the day-to-day operations but is a subject matter expert and is heavily involved near the completion of the project.

Class Assignment

Using the case study above, build a Stakeholder Register.

Step 1: List stakeholders

In Table 2.3, write the names and titles of each stakeholder in the appropriate columns. Using the description provided with each stakeholder listing, e.g., Chief Operating Officer, indicate the stakeholder type.

Table 2.3   **Building a Stakeholder Register practice exercise**

Stakeholder Name	Title	Responsibility	Type (Primary or Secondary)	Power/ Interest (HH, HM, HL, MM, MH, ML, LH, LM, LL)	Sentiment (Positive, Negative, Neutral)	Notes (concerns, priorities, expectations, relationship with stakeholders)

Step 2: Identify stakeholder roles and expectations

Based on the description provided for each stakeholder, use your best judgment to determine the various roles and sentiments at the onset of the project. You can start by asking yourself open-ended questions that force you to articulate stakeholder engagement, level of involvement, and interests:

- "How will this project outcome affect this stakeholder?

- "Will the day-to-day activities of this project create more or less work for this stakeholder? If so, do you expect opposition from them or anyone who influences their opinions?

Include any important information about sentiments, e.g., concerns, priorities, or expectations in the Notes column. The Notes column adds color to help the project manager generate the Stakeholder Engagement Plan.

When identifying roles, you can be specific, e.g., Lead Architect: Schematics, design, construction documents, bidding, construction administration. Or, more high-level, e.g., project team member, hospital employee. Ultimately, the project manager is accountable for the Stakeholder Engagement Plan and for ensuring each stakeholder performs their role. Thus, if providing more details in the Register is helpful, do it. If the project manager prefers a high-level snapshot, that is acceptable as well.

Step 3: Indicate the level of power

After reading the stakeholder information and reviewing how you filled out the previous columns in the Stakeholder Register, determine how much power each stakeholder has on this project. This can be tricky and is one aspect to monitor throughout the project to ensure you are engaging each stakeholder appropriately. Remember, you are assessing the power on this project, not the stakeholder's power on other projects or organization-wide.

> Write either high (H), medium (M), or low (L) in the power column.

Step 4: Determine interest

Analogous to the questions you asked for the Sentiment column, think about the role each stakeholder has in this project and what's "at stake" for them.

- Will this project outcome have a significant impact on their job? And, what about the day-to-day operations?

- Has this stakeholder expressed interest in meetings, updates, or decision-making? Remember, this is an educated guess at the onset of the project. You should re-evaluate throughout the project.

> For each stakeholder, indicate either high (H), medium (M), or low (L) in the Interest column.

At this point, each column in the Stakeholder Register should be filled.

Class Assignment

In this assignment, build a Power/Interest Matrix. Particularly for people who are more visually inclined, the Matrix is a great way to overview how each stakeholder should be prioritized. This Matrix informs the Stakeholder Engagement Plan.

Step 1: Review the Stakeholder Register

Referencing your newly created Stakeholder Register, contemplate each stakeholder's location using Power and Interest.

Step 2: Plot each stakeholder

Put the name of each stakeholder in the Matrix.

Remember, Stakeholder Engagement is about people. Each person may not fit precisely within a quadrant. You can place a name between quadrants if needed. You will learn more about building and analyzing stakeholder maps in Chapter 3.

2.5 Closing Thoughts

After you've plotted names in the Stakeholder Matrix, you have completed two crucial documents for your Stakeholder Engagement Plan. In future chapters, we will discuss how to determine the frequency of stakeholder engagement, the type of communication, and strategies to manage stakeholders throughout the project.

Depending on the scope and scale of the project, the project manager may choose to modify some of the steps when identifying stakeholders. However, creating the list of stakeholders must be completed to give the project manager the best chance at success. This can be daunting, but it is one of the most important steps a project manager can take to help ensure the Project Charter is met. The documents in this chapter - Stakeholder Register and Power/Interest Matrix - are tools that allow for transparency and strategic analysis of stakeholders throughout the project. These artifacts become reference materials in future projects and are essential inputs when developing plans to best engage stakeholders.

Quiz

1. **Which is not one of the four quadrants of the Power/Interest Matrix?**

   a. Keep satisfied

   b. Monitor

   c. Ignore

   d. Engage and Manage Closely

2. **An example of a stakeholder group might be...**

   a. Customers

   b. Community organization

   c. Employees

   d. Supplier

   e. All of the above

3. **A primary stakeholder is also known as a key stakeholder.**

   a. True

   b. False

4. **Project team members are an example of which type of stakeholder?**

   a. Primary

   b. Tertiary

   c. Secondary

   d. None of the above

5. **Where is the Engage and Manage Closely quadrant located?**

   a. Top left

   b. Bottom left

   c. Bottom right

   d. Top right

6. **A stakeholder can change where they are located in the Power/Interest Matrix throughout the project.**

   a. True

   b. False

7. **Which two artifacts are produced during the Identify Stakeholders step?**

   a. Stakeholder Registry and Power/Interest Matrix

   b. Stakeholder Register and Power/Interest Matrix

   c. Project Charter and Interest/Power Matrix

   d. Stakeholder Communications Plan and Stakeholder Register

8. Which stakeholders should receive the least amount of attention from the project manager?

   a. Top left

   b. Bottom left

   c. Bottom right

   d. Top right

9. When identifying the project team, which factors should be taken into consideration?

   a. Interest and reputation

   b. Skill and availability

   c. Personal relationship and availability

   d. Reliability and Interest

10. An internal stakeholder is someone who _____

   a. works outside the organization but is highly interested in the project outcome.

   b. used to work in the organization, but is not impacted at all by the project outcome.

   c. is a vendor that is crucial to several deliverables.

   d. are within the organization originating the project.

Answers	1 – c	2 – e	3 – a	4 – a	5 – d
	6 – a	7 – b	8 – b	9 – b	10 – d

Chapter Summary

◆ Identifying stakeholders as early as possible will allow the project manager, and the project team, to start the project with a clarity of roles and responsibilities, and to begin managing relationships.

◆ The Stakeholder Register is one of the first documents the project manager should create after the Project Charter.

◆ The types of stakeholders are: primary or secondary, direct or indirect, and internal or external.

◆ Details in the Stakeholder Register can vary depending on the project complexity, scope, and impact.

◆ A Power/Interest Matrix is a map the project manager generates during stakeholder identification and analysis.

◆ The Power/Interest Matrix plots stakeholders in quadrants (Keep Satisfied, Monitor, Engage and Manage Closely, and Inform) and serves as a guide for the project manager as they create the Stakeholder Engagement plan.

◆ The Stakeholder Register and Power/Interest Matrix should be revisited throughout the project and updated if needs and behaviors change.

This page is intentionally left blank

Chapter **3**

Stakeholder Mapping and Analysis

In Chapter 2, you gained a foundational understanding of the Identify Stakeholders process, explored how to identify stakeholders, and learned about the Power/Interest Matrix as one method for prioritizing stakeholders.

In this chapter, we dive into the various stakeholder mapping techniques and practice using each one by reviewing scenarios project managers encounter in the workplace.

Key learning objectives include the reader's understanding of the following:

- Various mapping options and how to build them

- How stakeholder analysis and mapping go hand-in-hand

- The different ways to analyze stakeholder maps and tips for identifying risk

- The benefits of stakeholder mapping and analysis

3.1 Introduction to Mapping and Analysis

Stakeholder mapping is the visual process of plotting the full list of project stakeholders (or groups) in one place. These maps can be illustrated in many ways, e.g., a two-dimensional matrix, cube, onion proximity map, or Venn diagram.

Regardless of how the information is represented, the purpose is the same. A stakeholder map reflects where stakeholders are at the onset of a project and gives project managers a tool to update when people change their behavior, attitude, or relationship toward the product or other stakeholders, or level of interest or influence. These maps are an essential component of a project manager's playbook, particularly as a Stakeholder Engagement plan is being developed.

Figure 3.1 **Summary of Mapping and Analysis Steps**

Brainstorm → Categorize → Map → Analyze → Act

Mapping stakeholders provides a way to visualize a diverse, and potentially lengthy list of people who are affected by the project. A proximity map (refer to Figure 3.2) is a way to display how close each stakeholder is to the project outcome. In Figure 3.2, each number represents a person or organization. Without a map, project managers run the risk of losing sight of how people relate to each other and how much energy should be allotted to each stakeholder.

Tip

Project managers can turn to collaboration tools, e.g., Miro or Mural, to brainstorm the stakeholder list.

Figure 3.2   Proximity Map

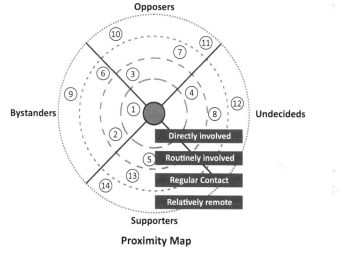

Proximity Map

Source: The Influence Agenda, by Mike Calyton (Palgrave Macmilan. 2014)

For a map to be informative, the project manager needs to gather information about each stakeholder. All of these details should be captured in the Stakeholder Register.

Whenever possible, commit to conducting a stakeholder analysis - first by identifying stakeholders - and dedicate the time to mapping before fully initiating a complex project. Stakeholder mapping and analysis will serve you well when you draft the Stakeholder Engagement Plan.

In Chapter 2, you learned steps, and what to consider when identifying stakeholders and creating a Stakeholder Register. Now, let's dissect the specific steps that result in a stakeholder map and give the project manager the information needed to adapt their approach and allocate their energy to appropriately engaging stakeholders throughout the project.

Step 1: Brainstorm

This is a method project managers use when developing the list of project stakeholders. This can be started by the project manager or in collaboration with the project sponsor. Remember to take into account factors like the business case, who is benefitting or potentially threatened by the project, and which people may be interested in the project deliverables. The goal of this step is to generate an exhaustive list of people who are considered stakeholders - regardless of their level of interest, legitimacy, support, organizational title, or power. In this step, make a comprehensive list.

Brainstorm Stakeholder List

1. John B. | CFO | high influence, high interest

2. Michelle M. | Supplier | high influence, low interest

3. Omar C. | District politician | high influence, medium interest

4. Petra L. | Business office | low influence, high interest

Depending on the number of people on the project team, whether they have been selected, and the sensitivity of the project, the project manager may choose to create this list with team members, the Product Owner, or project sponsor. Assessing the project complexity and other variables, the project managers may choose a more informal approach to listing stakeholder names or a more robust Stakeholder Register.

Step 2: Categorize

This is the step where you organize stakeholders into groups or types. Examples of groups are vendors, employees, C-suite, and community members. When categorizing using Types, you may include Primary, Secondary, Direct, and Indirect stakeholders. If you are building a Stakeholder Register, these categories are added to the Group or Type column. If you are brainstorming a list, you may elect to color code the Group or Type, or add it to the list item.

A key component in this step is information gathering. This needs to happen before the handoff to prioritization because this is where the project manager seeks to understand motivations, interests, levels of influence, and other factors that contribute to how a stakeholder is viewed and engaged with the project. When learning about stakeholders through interviews, horizon scanning, surveys, or other methods, e.g., brainwriting, the project manager should seek information about stakeholder attitudes, interest, power, impact, expectations/needs, and influence. Remember, these are in the context of a single project. A person may have a significant influence on Project A, but not on Project B. And, the project manager should be careful when making assumptions based on a stakeholder's title in an organization.

When bucketing and assessing people's anticipated level of engagement, motivations and lenses someone brings to a project are important to note. A "lens" is how someone sees the world. It is an amalgam of factors, such as personal experiences and environmental factors, that shape a person's perspective. Lenses are essential to acknowledge, not only because it is part of developing empathy, but because these lenses reflect how someone processes information, harbors bias, approaches situations, and interprets behaviors.

When it comes to what drives their interest, these are a few a project manager might encounter.

- **Political:** This can refer to organizational politics or external political interests. Will the stakeholder's organizational clout be impacted?

- **Economic:** Will the stakeholder be affected financially? An example would be a vendor or supplier making money from the project. Alternatively, it could mean a stakeholder is investing financial resources and is hoping for a particular return on investment. Included here is socio-economic interest. A lens that someone can bring relates to their socioeconomic experience or motivations.

- **Business:** How will this project outcome impact the stakeholder's role in the organization? Does the stakeholder anticipate gaining or losing something from this project? Self-preservation is included in this "business" interest.

- **Demographics:** Age, income, race, and ethnicity can weigh heavily on a stakeholder's mind and shape their perspective about the project.

- **Values:** Are stakeholders' religious beliefs, moral viewpoints, and values a factor for this project? For example, the company initiated a project to add gender-neutral bathrooms.

As you continue to bolster the Stakeholder Register with stakeholder details, it may look like Table 3.1.

Table 3.1 **Stakeholder Register**

Name	Responsibility	Type (primary or secondary)	Power/ Interest (HH, HM, HL, MM, MH, ML, LH, LM, LL)	Sentiment (Positive, Negative, Neutral)	Current Engagement (unaware, resistant, neutral, supportive, leading)	Desired Engagement (unaware, resistant, neutral, supportive, leading)
John B.	Product Owner, Resource advocate	P	HH	P	Aware/ neutral	Aware/ leading
Michelle M.	Provide product supplies, manage supply chain	S	HL	P	Unaware	Aware/ neutral
Omar C.	Public Affairs	P	HM	Neu	Aware/ resistant	Aware/ supportive
Petra L.	Primary product user	P	LH	P	Aware/ supportive	Aware/ leading

Tip

Think about the future. If there is information you may need, make a column in the Stakeholder Register or engagement analysis. You can always filter or create a pivot table.

Projects are anything but predictable and "cookie-cutter" so another way a project manager can bring stakeholder interest into focus is illustrated in Table 3.2.

Table 3.2   **Stakeholder Interest table**

Stakeholder Interest	Political	Economic	Business
John B.	▪ ▪ ▪ ▪	▪ ▪ ▪ ▪	▪ ▪ ▪ ▪
Michelle M.	▪ ▪ ▪ ▪	▪ ▪ ▪ ▪ ▪	▪ ▪ ▪ ▪
Omar C.	▪ ▪ ▪ ▪	▪ ▪ ▪ ▪	▪ ▪ ▪ ▪ ▪
Petra L.	▪ ▪ ▪ ▪	▪ ▪ ▪ ▪ ▪	▪ ▪ ▪ ▪

Step 3: Map

This is really where the mapping happens. When you are at the mapping step, stakeholder analysis has already begun, but it is far from complete. When the list of stakeholders is brainstormed and generated, that is part of stakeholder analysis. Now the question is: how will these insights be visualized?

Deciding which mapping technique to use depends on several factors. A project manager can work on this alone or alongside the project team.

- What is the size of your stakeholder list?

- How much do you know about the stakeholders at this stage of the project? (Remember, you should revisit the stakeholder map throughout the project life cycle and make updates as needed.)

- How much time can you allocate to mapping?

- How complex do you feel the map needs to be so the Stakeholder Engagement plan can be created?

- What are the questions I am trying to answer with this mapping?

The previously generated stakeholder list is now plotted - commonly a two-dimensional Power/Interest matrix. Using the names from Table 3.2, your matrix may look like Figure 3.3. In the next section, you will learn about the various visualization techniques.

Figure 3.3 **Power/Interest Matrix**

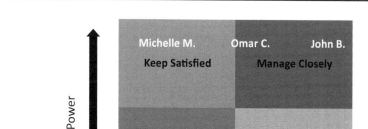

A stakeholder list along with gathering at least some information about stakeholders, even if it is based on assumptions, are dependencies for prioritizing stakeholders; so if these steps are missed, go back and complete these before trying to prioritize. It is essential to know who, whether by group or name, needs to be included in a stakeholder map.

Step 4: Analyze

The truth is that each of these steps requires a level of analysis. However, a step is specifically called out between Analyze and Act because this is when the project manager needs to look at the full picture. What story is being told? What is the stakeholder map telling you?

Several questions to ask when analyzing the stakeholder map are:

- How do stakeholders relate to one another?

- How many people need to be closely monitored vs kept informed?

- Do any of these stakeholders need to change their level of engagement during this project?

- Where do you see potential or clear obstacles?

- Who are your greatest advocates? Do they have a relationship with a stakeholder who needs to be moved to the high-interest quadrant?

Class Activity

In addition to the list of questions above, what else could you ask when analyzing the stakeholder map? Keep in mind that you also have a Stakeholder Register with information about each stakeholder.

Step 5: Act

During this step, the project manager, often in collaboration with team members or the Executive Sponsor, uses their analysis to draft a Stakeholder Engagement Plan. This plan might take the form of a single-page document that outlines how stakeholders will receive communication, which meetings are needed, the applicable milestones, and the types of updates people in each quadrant should receive. This plan also includes a Responsibility Assignment Matrix (RACI) and indicates how to solicit feedback and approvals from stakeholders. The contents of the Stakeholder Engagement Plan are detailed in Chapter 6.

 Class Activity

You are the project manager and begin a project by brainstorming a list of stakeholders and conducting interviews to understand their expectations, attitudes, and interest. You select a straightforward, two-dimension Power/Interest Matrix to visualize this stakeholder information. You create the map and allocate the time to analyze it so you can draft a Stakeholder Engagement Plan. As you are working on the analysis, the Executive Sponsor calls to tell you that the project is taking too long to get off the ground and shares their impatience with "not seeing any movement." Immediately, you pull the project team together and begin laying out milestones and mobilizing resources for the project deliverables. You are off to the races and never revisit your stakeholder map.

If you create a map, but never analyze it, was it worth creating at all? Discuss why or why not.

Case Study

On Juneteenth, Candy Stripe Hospital recently initiated a multi-phased initiative to create a culture that fosters diversity, equity, inclusion, and belonging. This hospital-wide campaign is the vision of the Chief Executive Officer, Sergio, who sees this as both a business imperative and "the right thing to do" to ensure that employees are able to bring their true selves to the workplace. Sergio is from a long line of educators and believes in the power of teaching others. Sergio is multiracial and speaks English, Spanish, and Arabic.

Chief Operating Officer, **John**, sees a direct correlation between a supportive, inclusive environment and employee recruitment and retention. John is a first-generation American who comes from a family of healthcare professionals.

Kathy is a nurse in the intensive care unit who has a background in pediatrics. She comes from a military family and has lived all over the world. She is married to a United States Marine who is currently deployed and Kathy is set to retire in three years.

Oscar is the lead project manager for each phase of this initiative. He has been at Candy Stripe for 12 years. Prior to that, he worked for engineering companies and in the technology sector. Oscar is in his late 30s, is married, and has a daughter with disabilities. Oscar has dual citizenship in Brazil and the United States.

The stakeholders listed above represent some of the key stakeholders, but there are dozens more including patients, Human Resources staff, and physicians.

The Phase I project charter scope includes:

- Identification and assessment of walkways, wayfinding, and signage.

- Usability testing and analysis of hospital technologies, e.g., website, registration and electronic medical record processes, physician scheduling software.

- Employee education around accessibility best practices

- Hospital-wide retreats focused on diversity, equity, and inclusion.

Discussion

1. Using the description of "lenses," brainstorm how Kathy might react to finding out about the hospital-wide retreats.

2. Given Oscar's background and life experiences, how might this shape how he views this project phase's scope of work?

The instructor can group students into two groups - one assigned to Kathy and the other to Oscar.

3.2 Types of Stakeholder Maps

Stakeholder maps are a project manager's window into stakeholder behavior and these maps offer a comparative view that helps inform the Stakeholder Engagement and Communications Management plans. There are several models available and a project manager should weigh their current situation when determining which technique to use.

Some items to consider are:

- How much time and effort can be committed to mapping and analysis?

- How many stakeholders are listed and how are they categorized, e.g., primary, external, internal, etc.

- Does this project require a Stakeholder Engagement Plan? Or, only a Communications Management Plan?

- How much access does the project manager have to stakeholders? Are they able to ask questions through interviews, informal or formal interactions, and conversations with people who know the stakeholder(s) to adequately assess each stakeholder's level of interest, power, influence, expectations, urgency, and legitimacy?

- What does the project manager truly need to know in order to move to the next step in the process? This may be adding more detail to a Stakeholder Register, drafting a Stakeholder Engagement Plan, or creating a Communications Management Plan.

- Ideally, every column of the Stakeholder Register should be filled out for each stakeholder, but if that is not possible given time, resource, or access constraints, include as much as possible and keep moving forward. Remember, the Stakeholder Register, map, Communications, and Stakeholder Engagement Plans should be revisited multiple times throughout the project life cycle so there will be more opportunities to add details and adjust as stakeholder behavior evolves. In Chapter 7, we will cover managing and monitoring stakeholder engagement.

In project management, there are visualization techniques that are more common than others. The Power/Interest Matrix and the Salience Model are ones that project managers are likely to encounter and use in their stakeholder mapping. A project manager should think about the question they seek to answer. The answers should also be available in the Stakeholder Register through sorting the columns or creating pivot tables, but mapping techniques more visually illustrate stakeholder relationships, their involvement, and their influence.

Case Study

Annette is the project manager for a project that is expected to take two months to complete. The scope is narrow and focused - to digitize Human Resource documents. The stakeholders are the Chief Human Resources Officer (CHRO), Human Resources Manager, Information Technology Director, Software Applications Developer, and Human Resources Administrative Assistant. Annette is in the Project Management Office, which is located on the same floor as Human Resources. Each of the HR stakeholders works on-site with the exception of the CHRO who has a hybrid (on-site and remote) schedule particularly because she travels frequently for the organization and is a sought-after industry speaker.

The Applications Developer is a remote employee who lives in a different time zone. Luckily, the time difference is only 3-hours, but this can pose a challenge for Annette when she's navigating feedback and juggling deadlines. All stakeholders are able to collaborate on web conference calls. The Information Technology Director is available by appointment only, but his administrative assistant is quick to respond to meeting requests. The stakeholders listed are considered key stakeholders with medium/high power and low/high interest.

> Does Annette appear to have enough access to each stakeholder or just certain types? Why or why not?

Power/Interest Matrix

This is a straightforward two-dimensional matrix that plots a stakeholder's power and interest in the project. Sometimes a project manager may see or refer to this matrix as the Influence/Interest Matrix. "Power" is used interchangeably with "Influence." Keep in mind that a stakeholder map should help inform how a project manager engages with stakeholders. Thus, the quadrants in this Matrix (Figure 3.4) reflect how to prioritize people.

Figure 3.4   **Power/Interest Matrix**

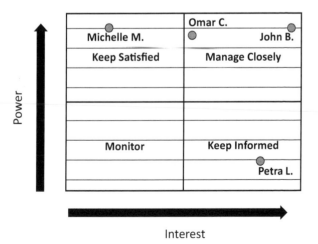

Sometimes project managers will categorize stakeholders into groups instead of by a person's name. Figure 3.5 illustrates how these groups can be plotted to inform the Stakeholder Engagement and Communications Management plans.

Figure 3.5 **Stakeholder Group Power/Interest Matrix**

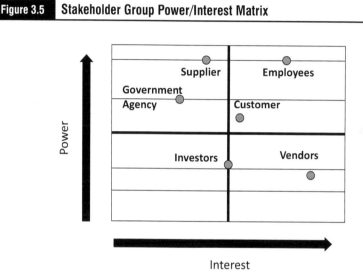

A third way to plot stakeholders with Power/Interest as the two primary measurements are to add "impact" or "importance." This is illustrated in Figure 3.6 with different size circles. Adding this data point further helps the project manager with analyzing stakeholders and proposing communications and engagement strategies.

Figure 3.6 **Stakeholder Group Power/Interest Matrix with Importance**

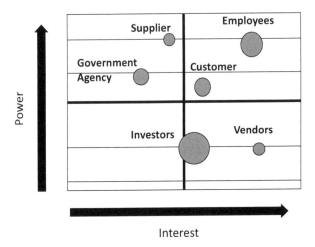

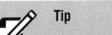

Tip

Be on the lookout for risk. Below are several ways to quickly identify risk when looking at your Power/Interest Matrix.

- A stakeholder group that is critical to project success has low interest.

- A majority of stakeholders are in the high power, high-interest category. This is a risk particularly if those stakeholder groups disagree during the project. Role clarity becomes even more crucial from the onset.

- A stakeholder group that is not critical or particularly relevant to the project has high power, high interest.

Awareness/Attitude Matrix

This visualization shows stakeholders' level of awareness alongside their sentiment toward the project. The project manager acquires these insights during the Brainstorm step when stakeholder interviews and information gathering take place. A table with these details should also be available in the Stakeholder Register. However, like other mapping techniques, a benefit is seeing how stakeholders relate to one another visually. Figure 3.7 shows what the Awareness/Attitude Matrix looks like in our stakeholder example.

Figure 3.7 **Awareness/Attitude Matrix**

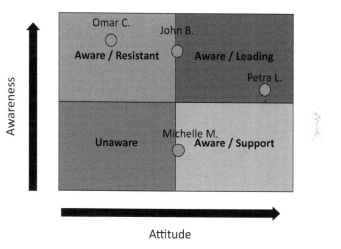

To make this matrix more robust, an option is to color code the Current and Desired state, as reflected in Figure 3.8.

| Figure 3.8 | **Awareness/Attitude Matrix with current and desired state** |

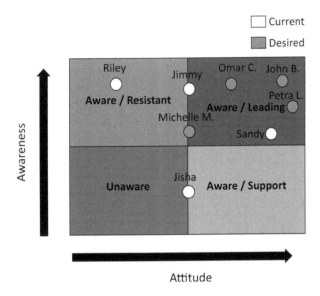

Tip

Be on the lookout for risk. Below are several ways to quickly identify risk when looking at your Awareness/Attitude Matrix.

- The majority of stakeholders are in the Aware/ Resistant quadrant.

- Key stakeholders are Unaware. Through an opportunity to create champions, this can also result in Aware/Resistant or require significant energy from the project manager to migrate stakeholders into the Aware/Support or Aware/ Leading quadrants.

- A majority of stakeholders need to be moved to another quadrant.

Salience Model

Expanding on the Power/Interest method of prioritization, the Salience Model introduces three parameters by which to analyze project stakeholders: Power, Legitimacy, and Urgency. These result in more precise engagement strategies and tactics that are tailored to each stakeholder. Salience is about the prominence and how noticeable or important stakeholders are to a project. The third area to assess is more time-consuming upfront, however, the additional parameter in the Salience model helps daylight "quality" so the project manager can quickly see who to engage and how to prioritize requests and input throughout the project life cycle. This is beneficial because loud voices can quickly derail a project or competing opinions can disrupt the timeline of the project manager and the project sponsor cannot efficiently identify how to weigh opinions.

To make this model worthwhile, eight categorization types should be applied to the three parameters.

To use the Salience Model, first, apply the three parameters, then prioritize people into one of the eight categories. Remember that the Salience Model helps prioritize competing interests and requests by seeking to determine who is most important and in what capacity.

Three Parameters

- **Power:** Synonymous with "Influence", power refers to a stakeholder's ability to affect aspects of the project, e.g., deliverables, or project goal(s).

- **Legitimacy:** This parameter can be difficult to grasp. In essence, legitimacy considers whether the stakeholder has a role and purpose for being part of the project or does the person simply want to contribute, but does not have a relevant function.

- **Urgency:** This is the stakeholder's desire for timely action. This begs the question, "how much priority or weight should be given to a stakeholder request or need?"

As with any of these stakeholder analyses, they are subjective. One project manager may perceive Stakeholder A as having "high legitimacy" whereas another project manager, or the Project Sponsor may classify Stakeholder A differently. This is another reason why it becomes critical to revisit stakeholder analyses throughout a project's lifecycle.

Eight Types

- **Discretionary stakeholders:** Though legitimate to the project, discretionary stakeholders have minimal urgency or power.

- **Dormant stakeholders:** People categorized in this type lack urgency. They have high power but are not legitimate for this project.

- **Demanding stakeholders:** As the name implies, these stakeholders are potentially high maintenance and can demand much of the project manager and team's time. Be aware of this type because these stakeholders have minimal power or legitimacy for the project.

- **Dominant stakeholders:** Stakeholders of this type hold power and legitimacy over the project. They can be loud voices "in the room," particularly around their set of expectations.

- **Dangerous stakeholders:** The stakeholders of this type are important to keep an eye on. They have both power and urgency but are not a critical project stakeholder. When project managers talk about a project decision changing directions or additional meetings to get everyone back on the same page, don't be surprised if the people responsible for derailing a project are part of this Dangerous Stakeholder type.

- **Dependent stakeholders:** These stakeholders are heavily impacted by the project outcome - thus, this type has both urgency and legitimacy. Unfortunately, Dependent stakeholders lack power so it's important to understand their stakeholder relationships and alliances because they need to leverage other stakeholders' power to get their voices heard.

- **Definitive stakeholders:** Also referred to as Core stakeholders, this group has the highest salience because they possess all three attributes: urgency, power, and legitimacy. These are people you want to identify accurately at the onset and manage closely throughout the project life cycle. Building relationships, engaging appropriately, and understanding the expectations of these Definitive stakeholders can make or break the project.

- **Non-stakeholders:** People of this type do not have legitimacy, power, or urgency for this project. In some cases, they may have relationships with stakeholders in other types, but in general, these people can be mapped outside of the center diagram.

The Salience Model is displayed as a Venn diagram as shown in Figure 3.9.

Figure 3.9 **Salience Model**

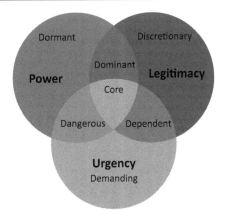

Non-Stakeholder

Source: PMStudyCircle

Let's take a look at Table 3.3 at how a project manager might input their stakeholder list into a Salience Model

Table 3.3 **Stakeholder List applied to the Salience Model**

Dominant Stakeholder HP, HL, LU	Dangerous Stakeholder HP, LL, HU	Dependent Stakeholder LP, HL, HU	Definitive Stakeholder LP, HL, HU	Dormant Stakeholder HP, LL, LU	Discretionary Stakeholder LP, HL, LU	Demanding Stakeholder LP, LL, HU	Non-Stakeholders
Petra	Alejandro	Jisha	Omar			Jeff	
		Greg					

Tip

Be on the lookout for risk. Below are several ways to quickly identify risk when looking at your Salience Model.

- The Definitive column is overloaded with stakeholders. This means the project manager will likely need to allocate significant energy to heavily engaging these stakeholders. While this is worth the investment, it should be accounted for when the project manager is tracking their own bandwidth.

- Anytime there are stakeholders in the Dangerous type, it presents a risk. The more names in this column, the more risk.

- Dominant stakeholders can steer the project - they are also the type of people who Dependent stakeholders rely on to make their voices heard. Because Dominant stakeholders can influence the project, they present an elevated level of risk so it's important to make these people champions.

Class Activity

During a planning session, the project manager poses an open question to a group of stakeholders. The question asks for feedback about a web module and for each person to submit their thoughts in rank order of priority.

Using Table 3.3, who's request should the project manager prioritize? Why?

Table 3.4 illustrates how a project manager can convert Table 3.3 into a grid that provides a high-level overview of how to engage stakeholders in each of these areas. This has shared language with the Power/Interest Matrix.

Table 3.4   Salience Model engagement grid

Engagement	Salience Model Type
Manage closely	Definitive
Keep satisfied	Dominant, Dangerous
Keep informed	Dependent
Monitor	Dormant, Discretionary, Demanding

As stakeholder mapping takes shape, so, too, will the Stakeholder Engagement plan. For strategic planning, the eight types defined above can be funneled into three groups: Latent, Expectant, and Definitive. The reality is that a project manager needs to balance the time spent mapping and creating Stakeholder Engagement Plans with actually managing the project. To assist with this, distilling the eight types into three groups expedites the planning process so the project manager can just develop strategies for three groups that represent the full Salience Model.

Cube Model

This three-dimensional model is a way to illustrate in one place the various stakeholder facets – interest, power, and attitude.

In this "cube,"

- interest can be "active" or "passive"

- power can be "influential" or "insignificant"

- attitude can be "backer" or "blocker"

Stakeholder **interests** are shaped by their motivations and lenses through which people see the world, e.g., economic, demographic, and political. This also applies to the Cube model when evaluating stakeholder "interests" in a project. When assessing how stakeholders are prioritized, keep in mind that interest is what they stand to gain or lose as a result of the project.

With **power,** sometimes it is spotted by the stakeholder's job title, but it is a risk to make an assumption about influence solely based on this factor. Remember, mapping is for this project.

Attitude is an aspect of this stakeholder analysis that can, and likely will change throughout the project as people are engaged and learn more about the project itself. Recall in the Knowledge Base Matrix that sentiment and awareness were plotted and in the Stakeholder Register, the project manager includes "Current" and "Desired" engagement.

Let's go through the steps to create our three-dimensional model.

Step 1. Understand how to create the cube as illustrated in Figure 3.10 where the Y-axis = Power, X-axis = Interest, and Z-axis = Attitude.

Figure 3.10 **Three dimensions in the Cube Model**

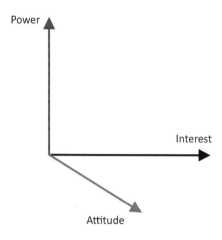

Step 2. Create the three-dimensional cube as shown in Figure 3.11.

Figure 3.11 **Stakeholder Cube**

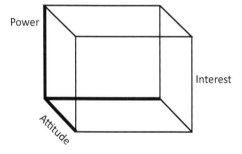

Step 3. Begin plotting stakeholder and interpreting what it means (Figure 3.12). The zero point is marked in red and indicates a stakeholder with low power, low interest, and a negative attitude. The further the person is from the zero point, the more engaged they are. For example, the purple dot in Figure 3.12 means the stakeholder has a positive attitude toward the project, but low power and interest. In yellow, the stakeholder has high power,

high interest, and a negative attitude. Finally, the green dot illustrates a stakeholder with a positive attitude, high power, and low interest.

Interpreting the Stakeholder Cube

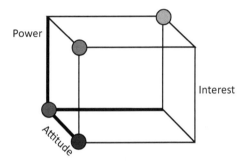

Step 4. Use the plotted stakeholder Cube to develop strategies for engaging the various types of people impacted by the project. Figure 3.13 articulates the types of stakeholders in the Cube as a way to remember what each person represents. This visual helps expedite the analysis and strategy creation to engage stakeholders. These strategies are part of the Communications and Stakeholder Engagement plans.

Figure 3.13 **Stakeholder Cube with name**

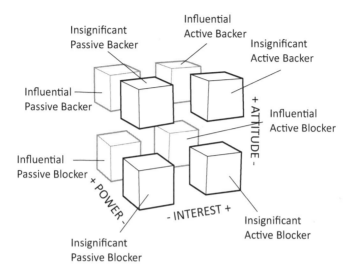

Source: PMStudyCircle

Tip

Be on the lookout for risk. Below are several ways to quickly identify risk when looking at your Stakeholder Cube Model.

- Stakeholders with high power and interest have negative attitudes toward the project. Keep "attitude" in context. Ask yourself if a positive attitude translates to support. If the attitude is poor, does this mean the stakeholder is a barrier? Are they actively resistant or simply not approaching the project with a positive mindset?
- Key stakeholders have low interest and a negative attitude.
- There are several "blockers" on the project.
- All the project "backers" have low power.

Stakeholder Relationship Map

In this section, we will explore the Onion Diagram, why it is used, how to create one, and what the diagram means for the project.

Unlike the other stakeholder mapping techniques we discussed, the Onion Diagram is a stakeholder relationship map. This puts the focus on how people interact with one another and how they impact the goal of the project rather than categorizing and prioritizing the stakeholders' impact on the project as a whole.

In short, the goal is in the center of the onion, and stakeholders are plotted in concentric circles around the center. Think about the phrase "three degrees of separation" when using the Onion. When stakeholders and what they exchange with one another - data, a sales handoff, steps in a workflow, and so forth - are placed in concentric circles (or layers), it illustrates that each outer ring depends on the smaller rings. The Onion Diagram is read outward - starting from the center. The closer someone is to the center, the high impact and importance they are to achieving the goal. It's optional to use the outer layer, but if used, this indicates the stakeholders who aren't relevant in the other layers.

When creating an Onion Diagram, the number of layers can vary - though four or five layers are more common. Remember, this type of stakeholder mapping is about visualizing relationships so use as many layers as appropriate to derive the right insights.

Creating an Onion Diagram is simple.

Step 1: Draw a small circle in the center of the "paper." This center point is where the project solution or product is labeled.

Step 2: Draw the first concentric circle. This is the layer closest to the center so the stakeholders represented in this layer are highly relevant and important to the solution or product. People in this layer interact directly with the center circle. Depending on the project, either the stakeholder's name or group, e.g., Business Office, can be listed.

Step 3: As the project manager and team consider stakeholder relationships to the center circle, it's likely at least one more layer will be added. This layer is used for individuals or groups that benefit from the center circle but do not interact directly. Consider this layer and additional ones during this step, keeping in mind what another layer might represent.

 Class Activity

The center circle reflects the core solution or project goal, the next layer represents stakeholders that interact directly with the center, and the second layer is used for stakeholders that benefit indirectly from the solution or product.

What might the next layer represent?

Figures 3.14 and 3.15 show several visual examples you can repurpose when mapping project stakeholders.

Figure 3.14 **Onion Diagram - Example A**

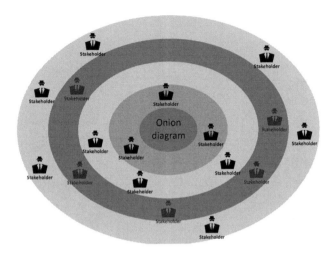

Source: Concept Draw

Step 4: Now what? The concentric circles are drawn, stakeholders are placed in the appropriate layer, and now it is time to map the stakeholder relationships. This is done by adding arrows, as shown in Figure 3.15, that include a directional sign to ensure a relationship is represented accurately. It is not uncommon for stakeholder arrows to cross multiple layers, including outer layers.

Figure 3.15 Onion Diagram with relationship arrows

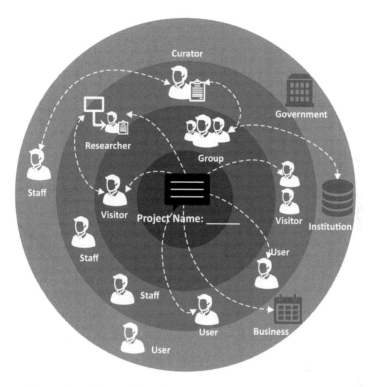

Source: https://www.edrawsoft.com/template-stakeholder-map.html

In addition to the arrows that indicate stakeholder relationships, you may come across or choose to include attributes like stakeholder attitude, which can be shown with color coding or a "plus" or "minus" sign. These attitudes are how a stakeholder feels about the center circle. If you need to analyze the relationship "health," this can be done by bolding or thickening the arrow and color coding to indicate a strong, positive relationship. For example, a strong, positive relationship might be drawn as a green, thick arrow, whereas a strong, negative relationship would have a red, thick arrow.

Tip

Be on the lookout for risk. Below are several ways to quickly identify risk when looking at your Onion Diagram.

- Stakeholders with direct interaction with the center circle have negative relationships with each other.
- The stakeholders that directly engage with the project solution or product represent a diverse group, e.g. a university might include "alumni" as a stakeholder. This is likely too broad and will not account for the segment of alumni who are directly impacted by the center circle. When this happens, break down the stakeholder group so there are more personas that can be analyzed and engaged with, e.g., graduates of the last decade.
- The Onion Diagram is misinterpreted. Keep in mind that a strong relationship between stakeholders does not mean they are more important to the project solution or product. This simply reflects the type of relationship between two people or stakeholder groups.

3.3 Mapping for Change

When change management is discussed in the context of project management, it could be interpreted in several ways. Someone may assume you mean: the process for submitting a change request or how the monitoring and controlling phase of the project life cycle accounts for managing change. The word to focus on for our purposes is change = people. As a Change Manager, these mapping techniques can be useful, particularly as you partner with a project manager on a project team. However, as you learn more about Stakeholder Engagement, you will notice how your particular role on a project requires different levels of attention toward stakeholders. For example, an important analysis to perform indicates which people represent the various CLARC roles. CLARC stands for Communicator, Liaison, Advocate, Resistance Manager, and Coach. Knowing which individuals are responsible for these roles allows the Change Manager to flesh out a People Manager Plan and Communications Plan. Additionally, change readiness assessment is another mapping and analysis that Change Managers undergo. This is critical to benchmarking where stakeholders of the change are at the onset of a project versus the desired state. Figure 3.16 shows how an Organizational Change Manager might structure columns during readiness.

Figure 3.16   Organizational Readiness assessment

Group Name	# of Assessed End-Users	Assessed Date	Awareness of the Change	Buy-In & Willingness to Support	Group Manager(s) Styles	Culture and Value System
Accounting Reporting Group	407	02-15-2019	Mid	Low	Consensus Based	Community Drive
Accounting Reporting Group	410	05-01-2020	High	Mid	Consensus Based	Community Drive
Analytics	204	02-15-2019	Mid	Mid	Bureaucratic	Bureaucratic
Analytics	315	01-01-2021	High	Low	Bureaucratic	Bureaucratic
Analytics - Regional	39	02-15-2019	Low	High	Consensus Based	TBD
Analytics - Regional	35	04-01-2019	Mid	Low	Consensus Based	TBD
Customer Mgt Group	2	02-15-2019	Low	High	Consensus Based	Enterpreneurial Mindset
Customer Service Group - Distribution	45	01-01-2019	Low	Low	Concentrated Power	Bureaucratic
Customer Service Group - Distribution	46	05-01-2019	Mid	Low	TBD	Enterpreneurial Mindset
Customer Service Group - Distribution	44	09-20-2019	High	High	TBD	Community Drive
Customer Service Group - Sales Operations	12	03-25-2019	Mid	Low	Concentrated Power	Competitive & Low Cooperation
Customer Service Group - Sales Operations	12	04-20-2019	High	Mid	Bureaucratic	Bureaucratic

Source: OCM Solution
(formerly Airodion Global Services)

As people encounter change, it is helpful to understand the Kübler-Ross Change Curve, and Figure 3.17 to help the project manager or Organizational Change Manager navigate stakeholders. People's participation and engagement in a project are ever-changing, but the good news is these behaviors can be plotted through their change journey.

Figure 3.17 **Change Curve mapping including recommended communication**

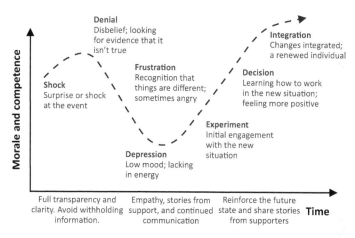

Source: Adapted from Kübler-Ross, E. (1969). On death and dying. New York: Macmillan.

As with all stakeholder maps, whether you are a project manager or Change Manager, these analyses need to be revisited throughout the project life cycle. People will evolve, behave differently than expected, and progress or regress during the project.

Quiz

1. **Which type of stakeholder map focuses on relationships?**

    a. Power/Interest matrix

    b. Awareness/Attitude matrix

    c. Cube model

    d. Onion diagram

2. **In order to analyze stakeholder legitimacy on a project, which mapping technique should be used?**

    a. Salience Model

    b. Awareness/Attitude matrix

    c. Cube model

    d. Onion diagram

3. **There needs to be _____layer(s) in an Onion Diagram.**

    a. 4

    b. 2

    c. 3

    d. 1

    e. None of the above

4. **Stakeholder mapping should occur as early as possible in the project.**

   a. True

   b. False

5. **Using the Power/Interest matrix, the paper supplier has low power, high interest. Which quadrant is this located in?**

   a. Bottom left

   b. Bottom right

   c. Top left

   d. Top right

6. **In a Power/Interest matrix, if a stakeholder has high power, high interest, how should the project manager engage?**

   a. Manage closely

   b. Keep satisfied

   c. Keep informed

   d. Monitor

7. **In the Salience Model, what are the three attributes?**

   a. Urgency, legitimacy, diversity

   b. Urgency, power, legitimacy

   c. Legitimacy, importance, attitude

   d. Attitude, urgency, power

8. **In the Salience Model, what is another name for "core?"**

   a. Demanding

   b. Definitive

   c. Dormant

   d. Discretionary

9. **What are the three types of Expectant stakeholders?**

   a. Discretionary, demanding, dominant

   b. Dominant, dangerous, definitive

   c. Dominant, dangerous, dependent

   d. Demanding, dependent, dominant

10. **Stakeholder maps should be revisited and adjusted, as needed, throughout the project life cycle.**

    a. True

    b. False

Answers	1 – d	2 – a	3 – d	4 a	5 – b
	6 – a	7 – b	8 – b	9 – c	10 – a

Chapter Summary

◆ Stakeholder mapping is the visual process of plotting the full list of project stakeholders (or groups) in one place.

◆ Mapping and initial plotting of stakeholders should be done as early in the project as possible.

◆ A stakeholder map should be revisited periodically throughout the project life cycle to ensure it is still accurate and provides actionable insight for the project manager.

◆ Analyzing the stakeholder map helps the project manager draft a Stakeholder Engagement Plan.

◆ Deciding which mapping technique to use depends on several factors. A project manager can work on this alone or alongside the project team.

- What is the size of your stakeholder list?

- How much do you know about the stakeholders at this stage of the project? (Remember, you should revisit the stakeholder map throughout the project life cycle and make updates as needed.)

- How much time can you allocate to mapping?

- How complex do you feel the map needs to be so the Stakeholder Engagement Plan can be created?

- What are the questions I am trying to answer with this mapping?

This page is intentionally left blank

Chapter 4

Stakeholder Engagement Plan

Before diving into the details of a Stakeholder Engagement Plan, let's situate ourselves in the project life cycle. The drafting of the SEP occurs in the "Plan" process. Docked to the project management life cycle, this Plan is created in the "Planning" phase. Remember, if the project manager is following *PMBOK® Guide* methodology, there are five phases, Initiating, Planning, Executing, Monitoring and Controlling, and Closing. Knowing where you are in the project life cycle is important because it ensures you have the appropriate inputs to produce the output for a given process. In this case, completing a Stakeholder Register and stakeholder mapping and analysis will improve your chances of producing a solid, actionable Stakeholder Engagement Plan.

In this chapter, it is pertinent to note the use of engagement rather than management because the purpose of the Plan itself is to *engage stakeholders*, not *manage them*.

The Stakeholder Engagement Plan is where the project manager applies the insights and analyses the data gathered during the Identify Stakeholders process. These learnings, along with a thoughtful vision for why and how to engage project stakeholders will yield a robust SEP.

Get ready to learn about and practice developing a plan to successfully engage project stakeholders.

Key learning objectives include the reader's understanding of the following:

- The purpose of a Stakeholder Engagement Plan

- What to include in the SEP

- How the SEP interacts with the Communications Management Plan

4.1 What is a Stakeholder Engagement Plan

A Stakeholder Engagement Plan is an artifact that outlines the strategies, tactics, and actions the project manager will take to engage stakeholders, gain and maintain support, and minimize barriers from stakeholders.

The SEP is high-level, yet directional. Depending on the size and complexity of the project, the elements included in the Engagement Plan will vary. Though at a minimum, stakeholders and their project responsibilities must be identified. A Stakeholder Engagement Plan takes time to develop and should be revisited throughout the project. To determine the most beneficial information for the SEP, consider the role of the person drafting the plan and what strategies are they pursuing. For example, your role in the project may be project manager and responsible for Organizational Change Management (OCM). Particularly, when resources are tight or the project is smaller in size and complexity, the project manager may double as a change manager. Remember, change management is the people side of change rather than the process of managing project changes.

If your Stakeholder Engagement Plan is actually in pursuit of driving change with minimal resistance then the change management model you are using will help determine how to shape your plan.

Regardless of the included information and the level of detail, the plan should illustrate:

1. which stakeholders will be engaged

2. their desired level of engagement and attitude

3. how these engagements will occur

4. how conflicts with stakeholders will be resolved

5. when the SEP will be updated throughout the project

For example, let's say you are the project manager for a marketing campaign. The strategies used to engage stakeholders might include:

1. Conducting focus groups to test advertising messaging

2. Administering pulse surveys to specific stakeholder groups

3. Asking key stakeholders to lend their expertise as subject matter experts

The more information captured in the Stakeholder Register uring the Identify Stakeholders step, the more equipped the project manager is when starting the SEP. These details about each stakeholder are important because ideally there are engagement strategies for each person.

Sometimes a project manager needs to make more assumptions than they'd like. Be flexible and don't let perfect be the enemy of good. Note these assumptions as a risk, and keep moving forward. Stakeholder engagement should be managed and monitored throughout the project and updates made to the SEP to help ensure optimal results.

Class Activity

As a class or divided into groups, brainstorm some possible engagement strategies for a Change Manager. Hint: Take into consideration people's current sentiment and their power/interest. These drive the engagement strategy.

Change Management Models

A prevalent organizational change management model, also included in the *PMBOK® Guide*, is Prosci's *ADKAR®* developed by founder Jeff Hiatt. Illustrated in Figure 4.1, *ADKAR®* stands for Awareness, Desire, Knowledge, Ability, and Reinforcement. To achieve the desired project or change outcomes, you will need to have strategies to move stakeholders through each of these stages in the model.

Figure 4.1   *ADKAR®* model

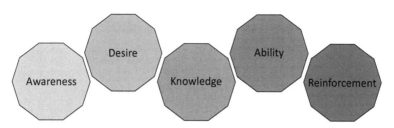

Source: Adapted from Prosci.com

Another well-known model, shown in Figure 4.2, was developed by Harvard professor John Kotter and outlined in the book *Leading Change*. A basic understanding of change models will help when drafting engagement strategies and communications plans. Specific attention should be given to building a guiding coalition. These people should be identified thoughtfully and stakeholder mapping and analysis should provide a helpful technique to assess influence.

Figure 4.2   **Eight-step Kotter model**

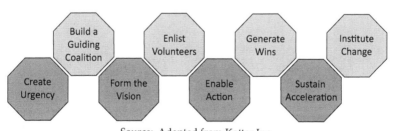

Source: Adapted from Kotter Inc.

4.2 Incorporate a Communications Management Plan

The CMP is a document produced in the Communications Management Knowledge Area. Similar to Stakeholder Engagement, the steps to create this plan are informed by insights from a Stakeholder Register, stakeholder mapping, and stakeholder engagement matrix.

There are several plans produced throughout a project life cycle, one of which is a Communications Management Plan. This artifact cross-pollinates with the SEP, as it outlines in detail how and when stakeholders receive communication, who gets certain messages and types of content, and what specific language should be used. The CMP is woven into the SEP and complements that document in order to guide the project manager and project team as they navigate stakeholder engagement.

It's important to understand that the CMP may be a component of the SEP, but if a project is small in scale and complexity, the CMP could live by itself without an SEP. However, an effective and robust SEP will include a CMP. The CMP serves as a project document that creates transparency and is actionable. It not only specifies how, what, and when to communicate with key stakeholders, but also includes all types of stakeholders, regardless of their level of involvement.

The CMP gets into the granularity of stakeholder communications and messaging so, in this plan, it's typical to include the "owner" of certain communication channels or types of content. In other words, it lists who actually sends the communication to a stakeholder group or individual stakeholder. This provides additional accountability, which is essential to making sure people are engaged appropriately.

When drafting the CMP and SEP, it is ideal that the project manager plan, monitor, and control all communications with stakeholders, but it is not always the case. Why? Stakeholders have professional relationships that may circumvent the project manager. Not only might people work together on other projects, but they could have similar job functions that cause them to interact frequently. These touchpoints provide opportunities for interpersonal tensions, and alliances (both positive and negative), and may lead to "backdoor" conversations about your project.

When drafting strategies in the SEP, the number of people you need to engage is important. The greater the number, the higher the chance that the project manager loses track of stakeholder expectations and lacks the bandwidth to provide the attention needed to ensure high power/high interest stakeholders are in good standing. In *The Mythical Man-Month*, Fred Brooks states his group intercommunication formula, $n*(n-1) / 2$.[4] Not only does this formula provide input into the number of people to recruit for the project team, but it also serves as a way to check whether this number of team members is beneficial or counterproductive. The larger the team, the more communication channels between people - adding complexity to what might otherwise be streamlined one-to-one communication. In other words, more people do not necessarily equate to more productivity. For the project manager, knowing the potential number of communication channels allows them to determine the level of team engagement that may be needed to maintain control and limit confusion among the group. The formula also reinforces the point that anyone can send communication.

---

4. Brooks, Frederick P. "The Man-Month." Essay. In The Mythical Man-Month Essays on Software Engineering. Boston, Mass: Addison-Wesley, 2013.

So, for 20 stakeholders, there's going to be 20*19 / 2 = 190 potential communication channels. Even if the project has a smaller number of stakeholders, let's say five, using the formula this is still 5*4 / 2 = 10 potential communication channels. This formula provides the project manager with a number that allows them to acknowledge and weigh the risk of managing a multitude of communication channels. Without this simple formula, the project manager may underestimate the risk and lose their handle on stakeholder communication. This is especially important for the stakeholders in the Manage Closely Power/Interest quadrant.

Class Activity

The project manager, Tony, just finished brainstorming the stakeholder list. After several iterations, he feels as if it is comprehensive enough to fill out the rest of the Stakeholder Register and map stakeholders along with a Power/Interest matrix. He determined there are eight stakeholders for this project, though he acknowledges this number may change later in the project.

How many potential communication channels are there in this scenario?

Simply from the sections above, it may be apparent that SEP and CMP are connected when engaging stakeholders, but how and to what extent? For starters, SEP strategies are often carried out through communications, so the discipline of creating a CMP that details messages along with channel and frequency is invaluable. Information in the SEP might also appear in the CMP or may only be appropriate in the CMP. The project manager, with consultation with the project sponsor and key stakeholders, can be helpful in determining whether creating an SEP and

CMP are suited for the Project. Table 4.1 visually compares both plans to illustrate common elements along with differences. Understanding these, along with how both documents interact, is helpful so that the project manager maximizes the time spent producing each.

Table 4.1	SEP and CMP differences overview

Stakeholder Engagement Plan inclusion	Communications Management Plan inclusion
• Current and desired level of engagement • Impact of stakeholder change(s) • Stakeholder mapping and analysis, e.g., relationship identifications • Methods for updating the SEP	• Messaging • Designated responsibility for communications • Methods for updating the CMP • Detailed communication cascade for specific stakeholders

4.3 Build an Engagement Plan

By this point, the stakeholder list is created, stakeholder mapping is performed, and the Stakeholder Register is populated. Recall that "Act" is an important piece of project management and the work done to this point should bring actionable insights that allow the project manager to efficiently and strategically engage people.

When the project manager is ready to draft the engagement plan, start by managing your own expectations.

Ask yourself:

- How many stakeholder names or groups are part of this project?

- Have you mapped and analyzed the stakeholder list? If the answer is yes, you will be able to apply this analysis when determining how to approach the SEP.

  - For example, how many stakeholders are categorized as high power/high interest or high power/low interest? What about Definitive, Dominant, or Dangerous? Be honest and objective. If there are five high power/high interest stakeholders, it is more likely the project manager can draft a detailed engagement (and possibly communications) plan to steward these people during the project. However, if there are 15 people marked high power/high interest, reflect on whether it's possible to assign certain stakeholders to the project sponsor or another team member to "manage and monitor."

- What is the size and complexity of the project? Is this initiative enterprise-wide, specific to a single business unit, or somewhere in between? Is the project budget in the millions of dollars or low thousands? If the project wasn't successful, what would be the impact on the organization?

  - These questions not only guide a project manager's thinking when drafting an SEP but are beneficial points to understand when enlisting the project sponsor or additional resources. Where the project sits in size and complexity can be helpful for resource negotiation and creating a sense of urgency for stakeholders.

- Has the Stakeholder Register already been drafted? If so, what level of detail exists?

  - If the Stakeholder Register includes limited details, e.g., name, title, and stakeholder group, have another honest conversation about why. As the project manager, do you not have access to key stakeholders? Is your project sponsor available and committed? Are the details sparse because of time constraints? This helps you level-set expectations. If the reality is that you have ad hoc access to stakeholders, minimal support from senior leadership, and limited organizational authority, then approach the SEP with that context. Remember, the SEP isn't about just checking a box. It is intended to be actionable and provide strategies to successfully engage project stakeholders.

- Do you have a thought partner who will develop and manage this SEP with you? Or does it rest squarely on your shoulders?

  - This type of situational awareness, along with the responses to the questions above, may determine when it's reasonable to assess and update the SEP throughout the project.

- Have you created an SEP before? Or, does this project have similarities to another one as a reference point?

  - Expert judgment - whether your professional experience or that of a team member is valuable when drafting plans especially when the people you need to engage are the same.

Additional questions to consider before drafting the SEP are:

- Which stakeholder mapping technique was used to prioritize stakeholders and does any additional mapping and analysis need to be completed?

- Does any information in the Stakeholder Register needs to be re-verified?

- Will this project benefit from an SEP or is a Communications Plan sufficient?

- What are my stakeholders' expectations, e.g., conduct daily stand-ups, town hall monthly forums, weekly email recap, or in-person check-ins?

Tip

Outline a vision for "engagement." What does this mean to the project manager and project sponsor and what purpose do engaging stakeholders serve? What level of engagement is needed for each stakeholder at certain points in the project? Openly discussing "why" the organization cares about engaging stakeholders with the project sponsor will help shape the SEP. If the sentiment toward engaging stakeholders is a chore versus a belief that engagement promotes buy-in and generates improved outcomes, this will shape the SEP. For example, if stakeholder engagement is a chore, then it's probably best to focus almost exclusively on people in the high power/high interest quadrant and deploy push communications to all other stakeholders.

To build a robust SEP, let's start with a scenario.

You are a project manager at Candy Stripe Hospital where you've worked for 10 years. You were recently assigned as the project manager on an 8-month construction project. The project sponsor scheduled an initial meeting to brief you on the business case and walk you through the vision of the organization's leadership team. Though this is a small-scale project compared to other construction projects, it is high profile.

As the project manager, you initiate the Project Charter (Figure 4.3), capturing the notes from the project sponsor intake session.

| Figure 4.3 | **Project Charter** |

Q2 2023
Project Charter: Candy stripe Hospital Employee Daycare Construction Project

Overview
This includes the background information and overview of the project at a high-level.
Candy Stripe Hospital prides itself to better the lives of others by providing best-in-class care in an environment built on empathy and inclusion. The leadership team finalized its annual and 10- year strategic planning sessions that resulted in several key initiatives. One of these projects is to create an on-site daycare for all hospital staff and physicians. As Candy Stripe continues to demonstrate its mission, this daycare facility should help alleviate the stress on working parents by providing on-site facilities and offering them a free childcare option.

Define the Problem
Business Case
The business case describes why this project is important to the organization.

> In addition to this initiative aligning with the Hospital's mission, it is a business imperative for employee retention, recruitment, and overall engagement. Candy Stripe will be the first hospital in its healthcare system to offer on-site, free daycare to all employees.

Problem Statement
This statement contains a brief description of what specifically is being solved for, what will be addressed. Sometimes this may be a problem that needs improved. e.g. process improvement.

> Since the COVID-19 pandemic, healthcare employees have been particularly stretched - personally and professionally. The industry has witnessed burnout and Candy Stripe has been attrition in their workforce along with heavy competition for employee recruitment. The Hospital must improve attrition wile offering a competitive advantage to recruit new talent.

Goal Statement
What is the SMART goal of the project? The project goal should be related to the problem you are trying to solve. SMART goals are Specific, Measurable, Achievable, Relevant (to mission/ strategy), and Time-Bound.

> By January 6, 2024, Candy Stripe will open the doors of a new, best-in-class on-site daycare for all its employees.

Scope

> **Will this project will likely need maintenance/operational support?** Y **N**

Luckily, the project sponsor is willing to brainstorm the project stakeholder list with you, including project team members. The list you two generate will allow you to identify team members and recruit resources by contacting that department's supervisor.

> In a working session, you write down every person, organization, and group that might have an interest in or be affected by the project.

Candy Stripe's division presidents	Communication team
Employee engagement council	Senior manager of public relations
Physician advocacy council	
City Health and Human Resources officers	Nearby neighborhood homeowners associations
Childcare accreditation governing body	
Local and statewide colleges for teacher recruitment	
State educator's board	Local politicians
Information Technology team	State lobbyists
Senior Director of Facilities	Local and national news media
Candy Stripe's architect	
Safety and compliance officer	Candy Stripe's C-suite
Jack	All employees
Jimmy	Human Resources team
Ben	
Dr. James	General contractors
Imelda	Kevin
Greg	Michelle
Dr. Roaquin	Jennifer S.
	Dr. Barto
	Dr. Lee

The project manager has flexibility when determining the details in the SEP. However, some of the staples are visualized in table 4.2.

To ensure you select the optimal team members, you create a Stakeholder Register with columns specific to engagement. At this stage, table 4.2 includes the information you have thus far.

Table 4.2   **Stakeholder Engagement Sample using Stakeholder List**

Name	Responsibility/ Role	Type (primary or secondary)	Power/ Interest (HH, HM, HL, MM, MH, ML, LH, LM, LL)	Sentiment (Positive, Negative, Neutral)	Current Engagement (unaware, resistant, neutral, supportive, leading)	Desired Engagement (unaware, resistant, neutral, supportive, leading)
Jimmy	Project Architect	P				
Neighborhood HOAs	No project responsibility, but HOA leaders need to be advocates and highly informed.	S				
Dr. Lee	Chairman of the Physician Advocacy Council	P				
C-suite	This group needs to be visible champions and buy into the vision.	P				

After conducting interviews and reaching out to project team members, you begin to understand their needs, concerns, sentiments, and interest in this project. This data helps you fill in the Power/Interest, Sentiment, and Current Engagement columns. To help visualize your stakeholders and how you will begin to engage them throughout the project, you select a Power/Interest Matrix. Knowing that stakeholder mapping and analysis should be revisited, you take the first pass with the information you've gathered, as shown in Table 4.3. As you interact with the appropriate stakeholders and assess their behavior throughout the project, you may add a relationship diagram, utilize the Salience Model, or include larger dots in the Power/Interest Matrix indicating importance. For now, the Power/Interest Matrix meets your needs.

Remember, whether it is a simple introductory email, a brief conversation with a stakeholder in the hallway, or a formal discovery meeting, everything counts. Each touchpoint is an opportunity to engage your stakeholders.

Figure 4.4 **Power/Interest Matrix**

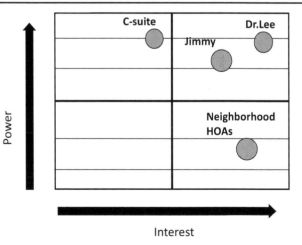

Table 4.3   **Stakeholder Engagement Sample after categorizing, prioritizing, and analyzing**

Name	Responsibility/ Role	Type (primary or secondary)	Power/ Interest (HH, HM, HL, MM, MH, ML, LH, LM, LL)	Sentiment (Positive, Negative, Neutral)	Current Engagement (unaware, resistant, neutral, supportive, leading)	Desired Engagement (unaware, resistant, neutral, supportive, leading)
Jimmy	Project Architect	P	HH	P	Unaware	Aware/ Neutral
Neighborhood Homeowners Association (HOAs)	No project responsibility, but HOA leaders need to be advocates and highly informed.	S	LH	P	Unaware	Aware/ Leading
Dr. Lee	Chairman of the Physician Advocacy Council	P	HH	Neu	Aware/ Resistant	Aware/ Supportive
C-suite	This group needs to be visible champions and buy into the vision.	P	HM	P	Aware/ Supportive	Aware/ Leading

Now that your stakeholders are categorized, prioritized, and analyzed, you have key elements of the project SEP. However, to design a comprehensive and actionable SEP, you need to articulate tactics and frequency of engagement, as shown in Figure 4.5. If you are creating a CMP instead of a comprehensive SEP, you will need the stakeholders by the audience, e.g., neighborhood HOA, physicians, and employees along with the "What's in it for Them" and "Communication" sections. Some of these tactics and frequency will be assumptions, but as you Manage and Monitor stakeholder engagement, you will adjust according to people's needs at the right moment in the project.

Figure 4.5 | Stakeholder Engagement Plan Sample

Stakeholder	THE BASICS			WHAT'S IN IT FOR THEM		COMMUNICATION		
	Power/Interest	Current Engagement	Desired Engagement	Primary Interest	Secondary Interest	Frequency	Channel	Purpose
Jimmy	HH	Unaware	Aware/Neutral	Designing a space that passes all city permits and surveys and meets the vision in the Project Charter.	Receiving compliments and gaining visibility with the C-suite.	daily	Meeting	All recaps
Neighborhood HOAs	LH	Unaware	Aware/Leading	Noise and traffic	General curiosity about how this daycare will benefit the community.	monthly	Zoom	General project communication
Dr. Lee	HH	Aware/Resistant	Aware/Supportive	Ensuring physicians' schedule and work is not disrupted by construction.	Does not see an immediate benefit in spending budget on a daycare for employees.	weekly	Email	Decisions update
C-Suite	HM	Aware/Supportive	Aware/Leading	Employee retention and engagement	Creating an attractive benefit to recruit and retain talented staff.	quarterly	Project Management Tool	Time sensitive information

Types of Communications

In Figure 4.5, you see tactics included in the Communication and What's in it for Them section listed for each stakeholder. These are critical aspects of your Communications Plan because it assists with messaging and tone that addresses each stakeholder's primary and secondary interests. As an optional element to add to the communication channels, you can include a more high-level view of the communications strategy, e.g., push, pull, and interactive. In the communication profession, we think about several types of communication with interactive being prominent post-COVID-19.

- **Push:** Examples of this type of communication include emailed status updates, dashboard reports to senior leadership, and video messages sharing project information. Push communications do not need active discussion. Rather, these are details that keep stakeholders "in the loop" and use mediums like email and report documentation that is more static.

- **Pull:** Examples of pull communications include ticket systems where people can respond to a survey, or submit questions, concerns, or issues at their convenience. The mediums may be the same, e.g., email. However, pull communications are somewhat unpredictable because it is at the discretion of the stakeholder when they will view, send, or share information.

- **Interactive:** People became exceptionally familiar with interactive communications during COVID-19 where professional environments leaned on tools like Zoom or WebEx to host meetings, conduct stakeholder interviews, and discuss project updates. Interactive communications are particularly helpful when the project manager is initiating and planning so they can productively gather stakeholder requirements, gauge expectations, and read non-verbal cues to draft the SEP.

There is no perfect concoction of engagement strategies, communications types, and frequencies because stakeholders are unique to a project. These communication types should be considered when drafting the SEP because a mix of each will be the most effective. Through the Manage and Monitor processes, the SEP will be updated to ensure optimal stakeholder engagement so always remember the SEP should not be static.

Ultimately, put yourself in the shoes of your stakeholders. Ask yourself:

- How familiar are they with this type of project? Have they previously been involved in a similar project? If so, are there lessons learned that can be included for this stakeholder in the SEP?

- What is their communication preference, e.g., email, phone, virtual meeting, daily or weekly digests? It may feel like each person has a unique preference. Whether this is or is not the case, the point is to tailor the SEP to the stakeholders, not to your preferences.

- What is their level of interest in the project? Do they offer ideas and participate proactively or does it take effort to generate engagement? Do they have the bandwidth to dedicate the time you need from them?

One of the best ways to answer these questions is to ask the person directly - whether in an informal call, formal interview, email outreach, or survey.

RACI

An RACI chart (Responsible, Accountable, Consult, and Inform) is helpful to provide clarity of roles to team members and to ensure the project manager and project sponsor are able to engage people according to the roles they serve on a specific project. An RACI is particularly beneficial when there are stakeholders who have organizational authority and influence. However, they are in a non decision-making role on a project. Illustrating this through an RACI is an objective way to articulate this role and reinforce it with the team. Figure 4.6 illustrates the role of a stakeholder according to an established RACI chart and specifically indicates the project task or deliverable associated with each person. This context is a useful anchor when developing and updating communications, and decreases the likelihood of team member confusion. In this example, we are following the *PMBOK® Guide* project phases.

Figure 4.6   **RACI Chart Example**

Project Name (link to charter)

Project task or deliverable	Person A	Person B
Develop Charter	R	R
Select New Software	A	C
Student Journey Mapping	A	C
	R	
	A	
	C	
	I	

Stakeholders have a "stake" in the project outcome and almost certainly will be dynamic at different stages of the project depending on several factors, e.g., appetite for change, and whether they believe the project will have a positive or negative impact on them. If the project manager, project sponsor, or any team member flags that stakeholders have conflicting expectations, are seen backchanneling, possess differing levels of urgency, or are not fully committed to providing resources, document this in the SEP and design strategies to tackle these challenges, e.g., one-on-one meetings approached with empathy, recaps that require acknowledgment of receipt. It is critically important to keep the project sponsor engaged throughout the project, as they are an influential champion with decision-making authority; so special attention in the SEP and CMP should be given to the Sponsor.

4.4 Create an Engagement Plan that Succeeds

As with everything you learned thus far, engaging stakeholders is a balance. Successful project managers need to use the tools and best practices at their disposal while considering the realities of bringing people along with a vision, motivating them to engage, and gaining buy-in that leads to desired project outcomes.

When crafting an SEP, remember GIGO (garbage in, garbage out). Invest the time to refine your approach to engaging key stakeholders, uncover "why" the project sponsor and your organization cares about stakeholder engagement, and give yourself the space to be thoughtful when collecting information that will inform your SEP. The more accurate the project manager is when identifying stakeholders, mapping and analyzing, and level-setting with key people, the better chance they have of avoiding "garbage out."

Quiz

1. RACI stands for_____

   a. Responsible, Accountable, Consult, Inform

   b. Reactive, Aligned, Consult, Inform

   c. Reactive, Accountable, Consult, Inform

   d. Responsible, Actionable, Consult, Inform

2. **A Communications Management Plan may be a component of the SEP, but if a project is small in scale and complexity, the CMP could live by itself without an SEP.**

   a. True

   b. False

3. **Awareness, desire, knowledge, ability, and reinforcement is an acronym created by _____**

   a. Project management Institute

   b. Prosci

   c. John Kotter

   d. None of the above

4. **An example of Push communication is_____**

   a. Emailed status updates

   b. Zoom meetings

   c. In-person meetings

   d. Interviews

5. **An example of Pull communication is_____**

   a. Ticket system

   b. Zoom meetings

   c. In-person meetings

   d. Interviews

6. **An example of Interactive communication is_____**

   a. Interviews

   b. Zoom meetings

   c. In-person meetings

   d. All of the above

7. **The Stakeholder Engagement Plan should be updated as a result of the Manage and Monitor processes.**

   a. True

   b. False

8. The project manager should ask the _____ "why" the organization cares about engaging stakeholders.

   a. project sponsor

   b. Most influential team member

   c. Community

   d. None of the above

9. The SEP occurs in which phase of the project management life cycle?

   a. Initiating

   b. Planning

   c. Executing

   d. Monitoring and Controlling

10. GIGO stands for_____

   a. Goals, initiatives, great, objectives

   b. Great, initiatives, go, onward

   c. Garbage in, garbage out

   d. Both a and b

Answers	1 – a	2 – a	3 – b	4 – a	5 – a
	6 – d	7 – a	8 – a	9 – b	10 – c

Chapter Summary

♦ A Stakeholder Engagement Plan is a document that outlines the strategies, tactics, and actions the project manager, and the team will take to engage stakeholders, gain and maintain support, and minimize barriers from stakeholders.

♦ Completing a Stakeholder Register and stakeholder mapping and analysis will improve your chances of producing a solid, actionable Stakeholder Engagement Plan.

♦ There are three types of communication that Communication professionals often employ: push, pull, and interactive.

♦ A prevalent organizational change management model, also included in the *PMBOK® Guide*, is Prosci's *ADKAR®* model. This acronym stands for awareness, desire, knowledge, ability, and reinforcement.

♦ A Communications Management Plan may be a component of the SEP, but if a project is small in scale and complexity, the CMP could live by itself without an SEP.

♦ Openly discussing "why" the organization cares about engaging stakeholders with the project sponsor will help shape the SEP. If the sentiment toward engaging stakeholders is a chore versus a belief that engagement promotes buy-in and generates improved outcomes, it will shape the SEP.

This page is intentionally left blank

Chapter 5

Stakeholder Empathy

Too often, Stakeholder Engagement is only approached mechanically – mapping stakeholders, establishing roles and responsibilities in the Project Charter, and strictly following best practices.

What's wrong with this? Nothing.

However, memorizing these technical aspects will only get you so far. The secret ingredient to successful Stakeholder Engagement is **empathy**.

In previous chapters, we begin your life-long work of becoming more empathetic by introducing Stakeholder Engagement, exploring why Identifying stakeholders is imperative for success, and outlining techniques used to learn what's on the minds and hearts of your stakeholders. Throughout this chapter, you will be asked to contemplate scenarios and practice seeing situations from others' perspectives through empathy exercises.

Are you ready? Take a deep breath, set aside your assumptions, and read this chapter with an open mind.

Key learning objectives include the readers' understanding of the following:

- How to define empathy

- How to learn about your stakeholders

- Techniques to practice honing your ability to demonstrate empathy

5.1 Defining Empathy

Let's start by defining empathy as the ability to take another person's perspective or imagine themselves in someone else's shoes.

Humans are innately able to be empathetic, but the activation of empathy is learned and developed. Genuine curiosity and an open mind will help you engage with people on a deeper level, resulting not only in stronger relationships, but in innovative ideas that are made possible because you took the time to learn stakeholder wants, needs, and feelings.

As a project manager or team lead, you need to show results. Know, however, that approaching stakeholders from a lens of empathy will help you with short and long-term success in your professional endeavors. Here, short-term success is defined as current projects with existing stakeholders; whereas long-term refers to your professional reputation for building relationships through a human-centric orientation. When resources are off track, the project milestones and deadlines are approaching, and a team member observes at an unexpected moment, you have a choice: respond transactionally or with empathy. As a professional, you have to *want* to develop your empathy muscle. Let's learn about the three types of empathy you can bring to a situation.

5.2 Three Types of Empathy

When psychologist Daniel Goleman offered his theories on empathy and its components in *Emotional Intelligence* and *Working with Emotional Intelligence,* he also proposed that empathy and emotional intelligence are essentially the most influential predictors of success in the workplace, but he likely was not thinking specifically about project management. As you become more self-reflective throughout your career, understanding types of empathy – cognitive, emotional, and compassionate – and how to apply critical "soft skills" embedded in emotional intelligence will set you apart as a project manager, project team member, and colleague. In Chapter 2, you learned that a stakeholder can be internal or external to your organization. Keep this at the forefront of your mind because these individuals may bring perspectives you can easily relate to while others will provide an entirely new way of viewing a situation or project. This will test your ability to practice empathy and, hopefully, push you to truly engage with all project stakeholders.

When demonstrating empathy toward someone, you'll want to be mindful of how you behave and respond. For instance, if you can only relate on a cognitive level, you might say, "I can understand where you're coming from and why you are feeling this way."

Let's look at some examples that you can apply to business relationships.

Cognitive	Emotional	Compassionate
This is when you can understand how someone feels intellectually. An example may be when your boss does not approve your vacation request. Your coworker might say, "If I was in your situation, I would probably feel upset, too."	Feeling an emotion with someone. This is demonstrated when you share a feeling of sadness when a person tells a story of losing a beloved pet.	This is perhaps the most obvious type because it is when someone has a desire to take action. This is demonstrated if you have been moved to donate to a charity because of a personal story.

Class Assignment

The instructor can ask the class to respond to each of the questions below or assign students to each of the three types of empathy.

1. Your colleague, Josef, has been preparing for a presentation for weeks, spending hours in the office finessing his PowerPoint and writing talking points on notecards. After Josef's presentation, he returned to the office and looked disappointed. Later that day, Josef shared that his presentation was met with tough questions that he couldn't answer. He said he was "caught off guard and stumbled in his answers."

   Applying cognitive empathy, how might you respond to Josef?

2. You are on your school's basketball team and the game is coming down to the wire. Thirty seconds remain on the clock, your team is down by one point, and you have the ball. Your coach calls a time-out to draw up the play, and you know Aaron will take the last shot. You inbound the ball to Aaron, he takes a shot from just outside the free-throw line and makes it. There are now 5 seconds left on the game clock. Your opponent inbounds and is forced to shoot from half-court. Your team wins the game.

Using emotional empathy, describe how Aaron may be feeling.

3. You are a supervisor for a team of designers. You've moved up in your career by working hard, investing the time to learn new skills, and having mentors to guide you. Despite your current success, your path hasn't been easy. In your first job, your supervisor would cut you off when you made suggestions in meetings and would edit your designs without listening to your rationale. You are in a meeting mixed with managers, junior staff members, and interns. One of the junior staff members recommends that the marketing campaign be discussed. Their immediate supervisor is texting and not paying attention. After the meeting, you pull this junior staff member to the side.

Using compassionate empathy, what might you say to this team member?

5.3 Learn About Your Stakeholders

In Chapter 3, you learned how to map stakeholders on a Power/Interest Matrix, create a Stakeholder Register, and identify the type of stakeholders on your project. Those aspects of stakeholder engagement are critical, but you need the whole picture to thrive in the workplace.

Tip

Someone's perspective is shaped by any number of factors including their current state, life experiences, assumptions, and values. This is one of the reasons developing empathy or "a heart" for your stakeholders is such an essential ingredient to project success. Stakeholders will interpret communication, body language, and interactions based on the set of filters through which they view the world.

It bears repeating in this chapter - stakeholders are people. They have lives at the "office" and outside of work – from navigating organizational politics to coping with family dynamics and balancing financial responsibilities. This makes your stakeholders busy and distracted. Like you, their time is precious. When a project manager understands that people have competing priorities, it changes how they engage with others. For example, empathizing with your stakeholders' lack of bandwidth should result in your emails being concise and to the point. You may even go a step further and highlight the main takeaways or action items to show you understand where your stakeholder is coming from when they say they "don't have time."

To demonstrate empathy, you must go beyond the Golden

Rule and operate from the mindset of the Platinum Rule. The Golden Rule advises you to treat others the way you want to be treated. The subtle, yet game-changing difference with the Platinum Rule is it asks that you treat others the way they want to be treated. If you work in marketing or communications, the Platinum Rule is hopefully a household term. If not, you are likely quite familiar with the approach of "meeting people where they are." This is another way to think about the Platinum Rule especially as it relates to how you engage project stakeholders. But, how do you know how someone wants to be treated?

As a project manager, you need to determine which techniques to use and how much time to invest based on where each stakeholder falls in your Power/Interest Matrix.

Let's explore ways to learn about your stakeholders.

- Brainwriting exercises

- Informal interactions

- Focus groups

- Pulse surveys

Brainwriting exercises

A technique used to rapidly generate ideas and, perhaps more importantly, hear from each stakeholder in the group, is brainwriting. This method is a productive tool for you as a team lead, project manager, or someone who is facilitating group discussion, especially when it involves vision or complex topics. Let's say you are conducting a kickoff meeting with the six-team members representing your various stakeholders. This is the first meeting with your project team after signing off on the

Project Charter. In the Charter, your team is asked to produce a digital-first solution that provides teenagers with mental health support services. You have stakeholders at the table ranging from teenagers who have previously received mental health support, parents of teenagers in crisis, counseling services professionals, web developers, and marketers.

Here's how your brainwriting exercise would work.

You would pose three questions to the group, e.g., What can we create that engages teenagers and empowers them to get the support they need? You give your group 5-minutes to write down as many ideas as possible. One of the benefits of brainwriting is these ideas are generated simultaneously and there is a balance of voices instead of hearing from only the dominant team members in the room. After the allotted time expires, you can either have team members pass their responses to the person next to them, pin them to a whiteboard if you're using sticky notes, or share these in a group chat if you're meeting virtually.

The goal is for all ideas to be heard. This type of exercise creates a feeling of togetherness and openness that allows people (giving your more shy or less senior team members the chance to "speak") to offer their perspectives.

In this example, your web developer may point out the imperative to build a solution with web accessibility standards in mind, your counseling services professional might share a personal story about confidentiality as people seek mental health support, and the teenager in the room who actively uses mental health services could share ideas that ensure a seamless experience because people who will use this solution are feeling an array of emotions, e.g., stress, anxiety, confusion, or loneliness. No single stakeholder in the room can offer each of these perspectives and a brainwriting exercise helps everyone expand their perspective.

Informal interactions

Informal interactions are another way to learn about your stakeholders and better empathize with where they are coming from. This is where project management with a heart comes into play. Your inclination may be to start the conversation with What. For example, how can this person help you produce deliverables on time, on budget, and within scope?

Stop right there.

Resist the temptation to use informal interactions like you're talking to a robot - a stakeholder is a person who needs to feel you are interested in their perspective and experiences. Begin by asking questions through a lens of empathy. Get to know the person on your team as a human being. Ask them questions such as "How did it make you feel when you were selected to help develop a solution to aid teenagers struggling with mental health?", "Have you or someone you know ever needed to access support services? What was your experience?", or "What do you hope to bring to this project and why?" These are questions that are more personal and help establish a human-centric approach to problem-solving.

Remember that getting to know your stakeholders is done over a series of interactions. Some may occur while you are standing in line at Starbucks, other times you might walk to a meeting together, or casually grab lunch. The goal is to humanize your relationship. You may be project team members, but inevitably, you will need to negotiate down the line so using informal engagements as an opportunity to gain insight into someone's frame of reference (and share what makes you tick) is invaluable.

Focus groups

A focus group is a form of research that pulls together a group of stakeholders for a discussion led by a facilitator. Using this approach to "get into the heads" of stakeholders will help you empathize with their needs and wants while also observing body language first-hand. A focus group is a good choice when you're seeking to a) hear directly from stakeholders and b) tease out the nuances of their responses to questions. Conducting focus groups yield insight into people's expectations, motivations and beliefs, and provide an opportunity for the team to observe body language.

In the situation described above where you are leading a team that needs to develop a solution to provide mental health support to teenagers, your team might decide it's critical to have more than one voice representing the "teenager stakeholder." This creates an opportunity to design and conduct focus groups that aim to help you empathize with these individuals and assist you in testing solutions to ensure you're achieving the goal(s) outlined in the Project Charter.

Pulse surveys

Repeated, short surveys usually conducted online are known as Pulse surveys. These are particularly powerful when you have a larger number of stakeholders, e.g., in higher education, you may administer pulse surveys to faculty during the fall and spring semesters. There are several benefits to gathering information about your stakeholders through pulse surveys.

Pulse surveys help you:

- Focus on what you're trying to achieve. When your survey needs to be short, it forces you to craft questions that get to the heart of what you need to know from your stakeholders.

- Spot issues or concerns more quickly instead of waiting for an annual survey

- Collect more responses. These short, typically 5-minute surveys, yield a higher completion percentage than lengthier surveys

- Gather data more frequently for continued monitoring and tracking

- Keep your stakeholders involved and help them feel heard

5.4 Active Listening

With any technique you use, active listening is key. The ability to demonstrate active listening takes commitment and practice. American Psychologists Carl Rogers and Richard Farson coined this concept in the 1950s, which may seem like eons ago, but was just the blink of an eye. Why did an idea to listen actively take so long to become mainstream? Perhaps it is unnatural for people to adopt the learned behavior of preparing to listen, being truly present in the moment, observing verbal and non-verbal communication, and providing acknowledgment and feedback as a result of the context. Perhaps, people are distracted, or maybe they don't care. Either way, a project manager will benefit greatly from this skill because it is a way to demonstrate attentiveness to others that builds trust.

Anyone can practice active listening whether you are the project manager or a team member. And, every interaction from kickoff meetings to random encounters in the hallway are opportunities to show you care. You can incorporate active listening into your life by doing the following.

- Nodding, smiling, leaning toward the person speaking, and maintaining eye contact.

- Asking clarifying questions

- Summarizing what you heard

- Listening without interruption

Remember, active listening takes practice. It can be particularly tempting to avoid the techniques above when you are working with a difficult stakeholder or someone you don't naturally see "eye-to-eye" with. This is where the "soft skill" of emotional intelligence becomes critical. It is not just enough to hone active listening techniques and study "how to be more empathetic." To establish meaningful connections with your stakeholders, you will need to pursue aspects of emotional intelligence, e.g., self-awareness and organizational awareness.

Tip

In a world living with COVID-19, the dynamics of the workplace changed. Active listening is particularly important for creating a culture of trust, open communication, and psychological safety when some stakeholders may be engaging online while others are in-person. Make sure to repeat back to someone what you thought you heard, nod your head if you agree, ask questions, and maintain eye contact.

Case Study

Throughout your career, you will encounter stakeholders from many walks of life. These individuals will "come to the table" with different professional and life experiences, represent a vast array of roles, and bring varying levels of interest and influence. Sitting here today, you may find it difficult to envision working alongside an insurance adjuster, a foreman, or a chief operating officer, but I can assure you that regardless of whether you interact with these stakeholder roles, knowing how to think about stakeholder needs is inevitable.

To start, know that empathy takes practice. It is a concept people spend a lifetime developing. You will not know precisely what someone else is thinking, but an educated guess will equip you with discussion points to validate and will demonstrate genuine interest that leads to strong interpersonal relationships.

Rules of engagement: Begin this next exercise by setting aside your personal beliefs and allowing yourself to observe every aspect of Figures 5.1, 5.2, and 5.3 from the role(s) you've selected.

The stakeholders listed in each of these examples are ones you may encounter for projects.

Figure 5.1 **Restaurant bakery**

Figure 5.2 Fox family

Photo credit: Sherwin Bartonico

Figure 5.3 College students walking to and from class

1. Using Figure 5.1, select one of the following roles:

    a. Nutritionist

    b. Public Health Manager

    c. Customer

    d. Restaurant Owner

2. Adopt this stakeholder role and carefully observe figure 5.1 - looking for cues that help you guess what your stakeholder is thinking or feeling, e.g., facial expressions, body language, and contextual details. Remember, you are not in Figure 5.1. Your stakeholder is looking at Figure 5.1.

3. Write down any feelings, comments, or questions that come to mind.

4. Share what you wrote (If you're working on this exercise by yourself, select at least two roles and reflect on the differences and similarities in what you wrote.)

    a. Discussion

        i. What surprised you about what others wrote?

        ii. What did you expect certain stakeholders would be thinking or feeling?

        iii. How did this exercise change how you view (Figure 5.1)?

5. Repeat these steps for Figure 5.2, but select from one of the following roles.

    a. Zoologist

    b. Park visitor

    c. Photographer

    d. Conservationist

6. Repeat these steps for Figure 5.3, but select from one of the following roles.

   a. Teacher

   b. Student

   c. Meteorologist

   d. Horticulturist

Quiz

1. **Active listening is important with stakeholders because it**
   _____

   a. Builds a culture of trust

   b. Is better than passive listening

   c. Helps you get promoted

2. **Which techniques are used to learn more about your stakeholders?**

   a. informal conversations

   b. focus groups

   c. pulse surveys

   d. brainwriting exercises

   e. All of the above

3. **Which one is NOT one of Daniel Goleman and Paul Ekman's types of empathy?**

   a. Cognitive empathy

   b. Emotional empathy

   c. Compassionate empathy

   d. Relatable empathy

4. **Becoming more empathetic takes practice.**

   a. True

   b. False

5. **Emotional empathy is the ability to share ___ with another person.**

   a. Relationships

   b. Actions

   c. Feelings

   d. Understanding

6. **Compassionate empathy goes beyond feelings and understanding. This type of empathy is about__.**

   a. Action

   b. Sympathy

   c. Results

   d. Feelings

7. **Daniel Goleman and Paul Ekman identified how many types of empathy?**

   a. Six

   b. Three

   c. Two

   d. None of the above

8. **Brainwriting is a technique where people write down ideas simultaneously in response to a question.**

   a. True

   b. False

9. **Pulse surveys** ____

   a. gather data more frequently for continued monitoring and tracking

   b. send lengthy surveys more frequently

   c. ask respondents to spend 20-30 minutes completing the survey

10. **You can demonstrate active listening by** ___

   a. Maintaining eye contact

   b. Looking around the room while someone is speaking

   c. Assuming you understand what was said

   d. Summarizing what you heard

   e. Both a and d

Answers	1 – a	2 – e	3 – d	4 – a	5 – c
	6 – a	7 – b	8 – a	9 – a	10 – e

Chapter Summary

◆ Knowing the mechanics of project and stakeholder engagement is a necessity, but the secret ingredient that will set you apart is developing and honing your ability to demonstrate empathy for your stakeholders.

◆ Humans have the capacity for empathy, but this skill needs to be learned and developed over time.

◆ There are three types of empathy: Cognitive, Emotional, and Compassionate.

◆ Techniques to learn about your stakeholders are informal interactions, brainwriting exercises, focus groups, and pulse surveys.

◆ Active listening is crucial to ensuring stakeholders know you are genuinely interested and that you care, especially in a workplace where interactions may be both in-person and virtual.

This page is intentionally left blank

Chapter **6**

Choosing the Project Team

Think of a time when you were part of a project team and chaos ensued.

Likely, thoughts also came to mind about why the dysfunction occurred. In this chapter, we will discuss how to choose the project team so each person has a clear role and offers the necessary knowledge, experience, and aptitudes to create a team that achieves project success.

You may be wondering why project team selection is included in a book about Stakeholder Engagement. All project team members are stakeholders. And, this "team member" group represents some of your most important stakeholders because they help the project manager get the work done and they are intimately involved in ensuring the project delivers value to everyone impacted by the project outcomes.

The project team includes the complete picture - the project sponsor, project manager, and team members. This means you, too, are a stakeholder. On any project team, the collective talent and leadership from all levels from the Sponsor to contributing team members matters. Team members are the key to a project manager's success - providing skills, insights, and resources throughout the project life cycle.

These key stakeholders have the potential to become visible champions or counterproductive adversaries and should be thoughtfully engaged.

This chapter also illustrates when and how to choose a project team, what to consider, and how to apply mapping techniques to determine who to select. Let's get started.

Key learning objectives include the readers' understanding of the following:

- What to consider when identifying the project team

- How to apply mapping techniques to team selection

- How to draft effective email communication

- How to respond when the team is predetermined

6.1 Choosing the Team

In Chapter 2, you learned some of the ways a project team is selected - namely by the project sponsor or the project manager. Regardless of who establishes the project team, it is a high-stakes responsibility that must be intentional and strategic.

Tip

As a project manager, remember that you are also a leader of a group of people. These team members are all working toward a goal, but don't always share the same behavioral norms as they collaborate on the project. This is where the project manager can establish guiding principles. These can be discussed verbally during the project team kickoff meeting or articulated more formally in the project charter. Previously, you learned that the Project Charter is a document that serves as a "contract" between the project manager, project sponsor, and team members. Being explicit about how people will work together, not only from a framework and methodology perspective but as team members, will benefit you and provide each team member with a standard by which to hold themselves and each other accountable.

The key is to develop these principles as a team, ideally at the project kickoff. If you cannot draft guiding principles as a group, then consider including suggested principles in the Project Charter for the team to review.

Here are examples of guiding principles your team may establish.

- **Equity:** We will consider the impact of our decisions across all stakeholders, and the potential disparities in impact for some more than others.

- **Stewardship:** Every dollar is critical and must be spent in ways that support and advance our value proposition.
- **Urgency:** We will make decisions with a sense of urgency, using the best available data, and a commitment to dynamic, shared governance.
- **Innovation and Iteration:** We will encourage innovation and embrace a "fail fast and iterate" approach with a commitment to continual improvement.
- **Future Focus:** "Because we have always done it that way" is not an acceptable justification for continuing a process, policy, or program.
- **Inspect What You Expect:** Honoring our tradition of critical reflection, we ensure that resource allocations and initiatives achieve their explicitly established goals and timelines. If not, innovate and iterate.

Figure 6.1	Team Guiding Principles Example

 Our Guiding Principles

Be authentic and empathetic.

Embrace being part of a team through trust and support.

Commit to lifelong learning that serves both personal and professional development.

Foster an atmosphere of creativity, togetherness, and fun.

Maintain high standards.

Promote an environment where it is safe to fail.

Be flexible, adaptable, and accountable.

If the team has yet to be chosen and assembled, this presents a golden opportunity to compile resources that can bring the most value to the team.

Let's begin with a scenario.

The leadership team in your organization, Candy Stripe Hospital, sets the strategic direction for the year at their annual retreat. As a result, several members of the leadership team have initiated projects of which they are now the Project Sponsors. You were recruited to be the project manager for one of these strategic priority projects. After a briefing of the overarching vision and project objectives from the Sponsor, it's time to get started identifying stakeholders.

Though team members are stakeholders and should be included in any mapping, e.g., power/interest matrix, there should be more emphasis placed on aptitude and attitude to ensure the project deliverables and goals can be achieved. Choose the most valuable project team using these steps.

Step 1: Define the "why"

A dependency to choosing a successful team is to define the "why." There are several documents like the business case and the Project Charter, that capture the "why" and clarify the problem being solved. Be aware that sometimes the Project Charter is created before the business case, e.g., through an internal project intake form or customer request. Other times, the business case precedes the Project Charter. The business case comes first when there are market forces at play, e.g., new industry competitor, that mandate that the business take action or there is a revenue-enhancing opportunity. Your business case can be developed in collaboration with the project sponsor and any subject matter experts in the organization who can provide the appropriate input, e.g., the Chief Financial Officer. Table 6.1 shows an example of how the business case fits into the Project Charter.

Regardless of whether the business case or the Project Charter comes first, the Charter should capture why the particular project is important to the business because this provides guidance in determining stakeholders, including project team members. This clear business direction enables the project manager and project sponsor to outline which individuals or groups are affected and have interest and legitimacy in the project outcomes.

Figure 6.2	Business case within the Project Charter

Project Overview

This includes the background information and overview of the project at a high level.

Define the Problem: Business Case

What is the business's need? How does this project address this need?

> In Q4 of 2022, Candy Stripe lost 20% market share in the New England region because of a lack of awareness and product differentiation compared to its competitors.

Goal Statement

What is the SMART goal of the project? The project goal should be related to the problem you are trying to solve. SMART goals are Specific, Measurable, Achievable, Relevant (to mission/strategy), and Time-Bound.

> By September 15, 2023, Candy Stripe will complete its value proposition research that will inform the creation of audience-tailored value statements and approaches.

No two projects are the same which makes it crucial to commit the time to clarify the "why".

Step 2: Analyze the project scope

From a team selection standpoint, the scope of work sheds light on the aptitude and level of experience needed to deliver value to the identified stakeholders. If needed, break the scope into tasks to ensure all skill sets are accounted for before choosing the project team.

This analysis will help the project manager articulate the type of skills and job resources needed to complete the project within the triple constraint. Resource management becomes the focus when the project manager completes an analysis of the skills required for the project.

Other aspects to consider when evaluating "team member experience" are the project approach and the role the project manager will serve on the project. If the project is Lean Six Sigma, then having knowledge of DMAIC (Define, Measure, Analyze, Improve, Control) will be beneficial in addition to the skills needed to produce deliverables. When the project sponsor chooses the project manager, they will contemplate the scope of responsibilities needed for this project. Specifically, some projects need the project manager to understand organizational change management whereas other projects may require a deep technical skillset and experience with a separate team member responsible for organizational change management.

Step 3: Identify staffing options

In any organization, there are fewer top performers than there are average or below-average performers. This reality makes these employees difficult to recruit for a project. When the project manager is identifying stakeholders at the onset of a project, make sure to note supervisors in your Stakeholder Register. They may not have a stake in the outcome of the project but are certainly impacted by the bandwidth of their direct report who may be selected for your project team. Now is the time to add these people, particularly if you need one of their star performers on your project. Resource managers are assets to the project, but need to be approached thoughtfully. These resource managers may be the Human Resources Office, especially for external resources, or department supervisors. In the case of supervisors, these stakeholders will likely be more protective and will need to understand the project context, vision, and needs in order to comfortably release or reassign staffing resources. A consideration for staffing is budget. As the project manager, you should work with the project sponsor to determine whether there is funding available for external resources and vendor support.

Step 4: Consider the whole person

In addition to availability, team members should be considered based on merit (skills), attitude, and power/interest. In this step, there is also an opportunity to create a map that illustrates stakeholder relationships with one another. If you can secure experienced or senior staff on your project, you benefit from their knowledge, influence, and organizational relationships so knowing how they stack up through mapping and analysis is important.

Class Discussion

Pretend you are the project manager and are working with the project sponsor to evaluate two graphic designers to join the project team. According to the project scope and complexity, both employees have the appropriate skills and a positive attitude toward the project. To "break the tie," you produce a Power/Interest Matrix where one of the employees was plotted in the top right quadrant (high power, high interest). The other employee was in the low power, high interest quadrant. Now what? If you only need one graphic designer, then the employee with high power, high interest will benefit you the most because they have organizational influence that can convert people to champions and help galvanize stakeholders.

In the scenario above, why might the project manager select the employee with low power, high interest?

Tip

If you considered two employees for the team, it is wise to make their supervisor aware because there may be a situation where a second graphic designer is needed for the project or the selected graphic designer gets sick, goes on vacation, or leaves the company.

Case Study With Solution

After listing the stakeholders in the Identify Stakeholders step, you decide to use the Salience Model to map stakeholders. The analysis reveals the following classifications: Karly is Dominant, Andrew is Definitive, and Sarita is Dependent. Recall the engagement grid from Chapter 3. All three possess the skills needed for the project team and are available. Which one(s) do you select to join the team? Saying "it depends" on your project sponsor won't get you far. Instead, think about the composition of the team as a whole - Karly, Andrew, and Sarita's relationship with these potential team members, ask the project sponsor if they have a preference you should take into account, and, of course, consider their experience and not just whether they "do or do not" have a certain skill set.

| Table 6.1 | Salience Model engagement grid |

Engagement	Salience Model Type
Manage closely	Definitive
Keep satisfied	Dominant, Dangerous
Keep informed	Dependent
Monitor	Dormant, Discretionary, Demanding

Author's choice? Karly and Andrew.

Dominant voices have the potential to derail or halt a project whereas Dependent stakeholders have limited power. They depend on a Dominant stakeholder to carry their voice and can be heavily influenced by this stakeholder type. So, adding Karly and Andrew ensures you have stakeholders with high salience. Whomever you choose, know how to engage them and how they can influence (or be influenced) by others.

Step 5: Refine the selection

When you have a list of skills, creating an Aptitude/Attitude matrix is a helpful way to visualize potential (and current) team members. A visual aid can be beneficial when presenting to management as well. Lean on the team's resource manager, project sponsor, and the employees' supervisors to refine team member selection. How many people do you need on your team? This truly depends on the project, though, there is a model from Amazon that is valuable to consider. This model evolved from the two-pizza-team rule developed by Amazon's Executive Chairman, Jeff Bezos. This rule offered that the ideal team size does not exceed the number of people who can eat two large pizzas. Though it is true that smaller teams are more agile and more efficient to manage, the key is to recruit the people with the right combination of aptitude, attitude, and availability to make the project a success. The evolved, more effective model from Amazon is the single-threaded leader team where team members are able to dedicate themselves to a single project. Creating single-threaded leader teams is not always feasible in an organization, but the principle remains – to ensure that team members have adequate resources and availability to focus on the tasks at hand.

Figure 6.3 Graphic Design Aptitude/Attitude Matrix

Graphic Design Skills

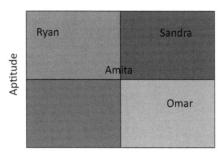

Figure 6.4 Account Service Aptitude/Attitude Matrix

Account Service Skills

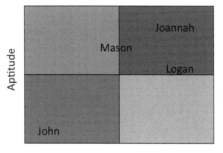

Figure 6.5   **Team member behavioral matrix**

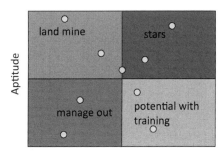

Time is a luxury not often afforded to project managers. If you are in a time constraint or pressured to "just select the team and have the kickoff meeting," then at a minimum, set up the Stakeholder Register and brainstorm the stakeholder list. Team members are primary stakeholders so this step is unavoidable. The mapping is important, but there are opportunities throughout the project to revisit this, especially when new information about stakeholders is gathered.

Step 6: Project team outreach

Now that your dream team is selected, it's time to recruit. What do you say when recruiting a team member? What do they need to know? Why is it important to be clear with these stakeholders? This outreach sets the tone for how this group of stakeholders feels about the project. And, it is crucial for these people to become project champions.

When crafting a successful email message, it is wise to be clear and concise and to check grammar and spelling. Having some insight into these team members' preferences and styles will also contribute to how you draft this communication. For example, if a project team member is an executive whom you've never met, you should be more formal in tone, remain professional, and consider incorporating bullets in your email. It's also likely that these team members receive hundreds of emails a day so including the request and deadline in the subject line can be beneficial.

Tip

Before reaching out to potential team members, set up your Stakeholder Register and map stakeholders if you have not done so already (see Chapter 3 for types of maps).

With any outreach, regardless of the team member, it is essential to know why you are writing to them and what action, if any, you need them to take, and by when. Especially when a project manager lacks organizational authority, there is a tendency to send vague communication for fear of being "too directive" to management. Resist this temptation. It will result in 1) a lack of response 2) a need for follow-ups and clarification 3) frustration. If there is a call-to-action, you want this to be specific e.g., Let me know by X date or confirm your acceptance by emailing me at XXXX@XXXX.com. Make the action item(s) visible and clear. This is a best practice for outreach and any email communication. Also, keep in mind BLOT (bottom line on top). What is the purpose of your email? State this in the first couple of paragraphs. To accompany this purpose, include more details in subsequent paragraphs to ensure someone can gain context. This will help them make more informed decisions and, if they have follow-up questions, these will be more specific rather than, "can you tell me more about why you need my involvement?" This is double work so be mindful to avoid such inefficiencies.

Sample outreach email A

[subject line] Your participation is requested

I write to give you a heads-up on a project that will benefit from your insight and expertise. You've heard the leadership team share its 3-year strategic plan at the recent state of the company forum. As a result, a project to improve processes, and develop shared language and tools across the company has been initiated.

[Name of employee], is leading this effort.

During the next couple of weeks, [Name of employee] will be reaching out to each of you to provide details and to conduct an exploratory meeting that will help inform a project charter.

I am excited about this opportunity and am looking forward to the results of this collaboration.

Thank you in advance for your support and insight.

Sample outreach email B

[subject line] For review by August 31: Project Charter

John,

Thank you for the productive exploratory discussion. Your insight informed this first draft of the Project Charter. Included here is the draft Charter for your review by August 31. This is a Google document shared with other project team members so please provide your feedback directly in the document for transparency.

Please let me know if you have any questions. Your input is important as we work to refine this Charter to ensure the milestones, timeline, and scope are feasible.

Once all feedback is collected, I will schedule a brief, 30-min session where we will reconcile everyone's comments and finalize the Project Charter.

Thank you for your continued partnership.

Class Assignment

Using the sample emails, craft your own outreach communication. Be prepared to share your email and discuss where you included the best practices you learned from the sample outreach.

6.2 The Team is Predetermined

If the project manager finds themself in a situation where the project team is "handed" to them, here are some considerations to make the most out of this scenario.

- Make sure to map these team members so you can see what type of stakeholder they are, e.g., Low power/High interest, Dominant, Aware/Supportive.

- Identify which stakeholders from the Stakeholder Register might feel they "should have been selected"

- Confirm any influential relationship between team members

- Note High power/High interest stakeholders and people with High power/Low interest that you want as a future champion. Just because someone is not on the project team doesn't mean they can't be in the game.

Whether the team is selected on your behalf or you have the opportunity to curate the perfect blend of skills and attitudes, remember that teams need motivation - especially if the project is complex or long in duration. It is a part of the project manager's role to keep team members engaged so they can give their best work and their best selves.

Tip

In 2022, I completed the Google Project Management Certificate Program and in one of the courses, Google conducted research that sought to pinpoint what contributed to team effectiveness. As a result of the study, they identified: psychological safety, dependability, structure and clarity, meaning, and impact.

This might not be the case for your organization, or your team, but investing the time to learn "what makes your team tick" will help set you, and the team, up for success.

6.3 Selecting the Project Manager

The project manager's roles and responsibilities differ depending on the organization, its culture, and the needs of the project itself. The project sponsor is either solely or part of the decision-making group that selects the project manager. But wait! Why aren't the project manager's job duties standardized regardless of the company or industry? Simply put, a successful project manager balances the tenants of project management with their ability to engage people. The project manager is the team's leader so their ability to run a successful project is far more nuanced than simply finding someone who can focus on deliverables, budget, and timeline.

Additionally, project managers have varying degrees of experience in employing certain frameworks and methodologies. In the end, all project managers should be able to "talk the talk," but what separates the good from the great are the soft skills and whether the project manager is competent in adapting to situations, navigating complex roadblocks, and negotiating with stakeholders. These soft skills should be heavily weighted when the project sponsor considers who to assign as the project manager.

Level-setting roles and responsibilities before making the project manager selection are critical particularly because these will vary. For example, at a company, we say the project manager develops the Project Plan with the project team and manages the team's performance of project tasks. It is also the responsibility of the project manager to secure acceptance and approval of deliverables from the project sponsor and Stakeholders. The project manager is also responsible for communication, including status reporting, risk management, and escalation of issues that cannot be resolved in the team.

At the Trinity University Project Portfolio Management Office Center of Excellence, our team determined the top competencies for a successful project manager. These are illustrated in table 6.2.

Table 6.2   **Project Manager Competencies**

Critical Competency	Definition
action oriented	Taking on new opportunities and touch challenges with a sense of urgency, high energy, and enthusiasm.
collaborates	Building partnership and working collaboratively with others to meet shared objectives.
communicates effectively	Developing and delivering multi-mode communications that convey a clear understanding of the unique needs of different audiences.
plans/aligns	Planning and prioritizing work to meet commitments aligned with organizational goals
drives results	Consistently achieving results, even under tough circumstances.
manages complexity	Making sence of complex, high quantity, and sometimes contradictory information to effectively solve problems.
customer focus	Building strong customer relationship and delivering customer-centric solutions.
directs work	Providing direction, delegating, and removing obstacles to get work done.
situational adaptability	Adapting approach and demeanor in real time to match the shifting demands of different situations
Values Differences	Recognizing the value that different perspective and cultures bring to an organization

The importance of communication cannot be understated. As a project sponsor, this is an aspect to consider when identifying a project manager and if this person will also be responsible for an organizational change management function. In Chapter 5, you learned about empathy and the power of active listening. This is a component of communication and is paramount not only for project management success but for building relationships for future projects.

Identifying a project manager who can lead and motivate a team to deliver a project on time, on budget, and on scope may feel like a unicorn employee, so use the tools available, e.g., an Aptitude/Attitude Matrix when making this decision.

6.4 Identifying the Project Sponsor

When a project has two sponsors, it should be noted as a possible risk. Unless the co-sponsors are in lockstep, it can pose difficulty for the project manager during consensus building. During project Initiation, it's critical that the co-sponsors determine the "first among equals" in the event the team needs a tie-breaker decision or needs confirmation of direction. As a project manager, determining the project sponsor is likely out of your control so be prepared to flex your communication and active listening muscles in the event you are working with a difficult Sponsor. You will learn more about working with difficult stakeholders in Chapter 7.

Quiz

1. The term DMAIC stands for _____

   a. Define, Measure, Assess, Implement, Close

   b. Define, Measure, Analyze, Improve, Control

   c. Define, Metrics, Analyze, Implement, Close

   d. Determine, Measure, Address, Improve, Control

2. When determining skills needed for a project team, a _____ is helpful.

   a. WBS

   b. Stakeholder Register

   c. Resource Manager

   d. Both a and c

3. _____ principles are sometimes included in the Project Charter.

   a. Guiding

   b. Vision

   c. Project manager

   d. None of the above

4. **What is the two-pizza-team rule?**

   a. The project manager has to bring two pizzas to the team kickoff meeting.

   b. Teams should limit their size to the number of people they can feed with two large pizzas.

   c. To celebrate, a team should eat two pizzas when completing a project.

   d. Both a and c

5. **Single-threaded leader team evolved from the two-pizza-team rule.**

   a. True

   b. False

6. **Google conducted research that sought to pinpoint what contributed to team effectiveness. One of these factors was____**

   a. open communication

   b. psychological safety

   c. professional relationships

   d. None of the above

7. Google conducted research that sought to pinpoint what contributed to team effectiveness. One of these factors was____

   a. dependability

   b. flexibility

   c. work environment

   d. food

8. Google conducted research that sought to pinpoint what contributed to team effectiveness. One of these factors was____

   a. other team members

   b. clarity

   c. structure

   d. Both b and c

9. When crafting email communication to team members, BLOT is an effective structure

   a. True

   b. False

10. BLOT stands for_____

a. Bottom line on top

b. Branding low outcome tasks

c. Be lively or tenacious

d. Both a and b

Answers	1 – b	2 – d	3 – a	4 – b	5 – a
	6 – b	7 – a	8 – d	9 – a	10 – a

Chapter Summary

◆ Amazon's single-threaded leader teams allow team members to only focus on one project at a time. This is not always feasible in an organization, but the principle remains – to ensure that team members have adequate resources and availability to focus on the tasks at hand.

◆ When crafting email communication, keep BLOT in mind. This stands for Bottom Line On Top.

◆ In addition to availability, team members should be considered based on merit (skills), attitude, and power/ interest.

◆ The type of project is an important consideration when identifying the people most suited for the team, e.g., if you are running a Lean Six Sigma project then a team member's knowledge of DMAIC is a plus.

◆ An Aptitude/Attitude matrix is a useful tool when assessing team member candidates

Chapter **7**

Manage and Monitor Stakeholders

Congratulations! You made it to steps 3 and 4 of the Stakeholder Engagement life cycle. This means the focus shifts to action (and reaction). In the Manage and Monitor steps, the project manager will engage, adjust, and re-engage stakeholders according to the stakeholder engagement plan.

In Chapter 1, you learned about the four processes in the Stakeholder Engagement life cycle: Identify, Plan, Manage, and Monitor. These final two steps in the relay can seem like an endless loop around the track because the project manager must react to people's behavior. And, people behave precisely as predicted, right? Of course not.

In this chapter, we explore what Managing and Monitoring really mean in the context of Stakeholder Engagement and practice ways to continuously evaluate and adapt to people's expectations.

> Key learning objectives include the readers' understanding of the following:
>
> - The purpose and usage of the Lessons Learned Register and Issue Log
> - How to continuously analyze stakeholders' evolving behavior
> - What to expect during the Manage and Monitor steps of the process

7.1 The Mechanics of Managing and Monitoring Stakeholder Engagement

Whether at a theme park or a shopping mall, a useful map orients the reader by including "You Are Here." Like a map, table 7.1 shows you which phase of the project life cycle Manage and Monitor Stakeholder Engagement resides.

Table 7.1	Stakeholder Engagement processes in each phase

Process	Initiation	Planning	Executing	Monitoring and Controlling	Closing
Identify Stakeholders	o				
Plan Stakeholder Engagement		o			
Manage Stakeholder Engagement			o		
Monitor Stakeholder Engagement				o	

In the Stakeholder Engagement life cycle, each preceding step is a building block. And, though it's unreasonable to ask a project manager to predict how every stakeholder will behave during their project, the more successful the project manager is at accurately identifying stakeholders and planning for their needs and expectations, the greater chance they have of achieving the sought-after outcomes. People's project needs and relationships with one another are dynamic. Therefore, the project manager should expect to adjust the Stakeholder Engagement Plan to acknowledge evolving stakeholder behavior. Sometimes, especially on large, complex projects, the Manage and Monitor stages may lead the project manager to revisit the Identify Stakeholder stage, thus requiring an update to the Stakeholder Register and Stakeholder Engagement Plan. Remember, the Manage stage is about managing your Engagement Plan so as situations arise or new information is available, the project manager should re-engage with any stage that's required to appropriately update the SEP, as shown in Figure 7.1.

Figure 7.1   **Building blocks of the Stakeholder Engagement life cycle**

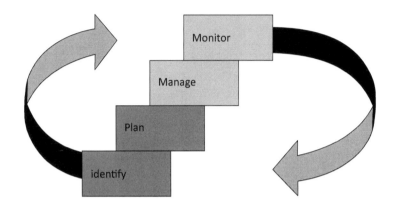

If a project manager possesses soft skills, the Manage and Monitor steps aren't as grueling. However, if the project manager's bent is more technical and process-oriented, the idea of actively engaging people and responding to their emotions is a steep hill to climb. Chapter 6 overviews the essential skills of a project manager which are mostly focused on these soft skills because it is truly what sets a project manager apart.

Class Discussion

Which type of project manager are you? Are you more people or process-oriented?

Back to the mechanics. Unlike the previous steps, by the time Manage and Monitor are in full swing, the project manager has several valuable artifacts along with tools and techniques that help them navigate this part of the process. The outputs for both Manage and Monitor are updates to existing documents. If these touchstone documents are left stagnant, the project manager leaves themself and the project open to increased risk of failure.

Take a moment to reflect on what you learned so far. Which methods, models, and artifacts are available to you as you fully embrace the final stages of Stakeholder Engagement - Manage and Monitor?

Some of these include:

- Project Management Plan

- Stakeholder Engagement Plan

- Expert Judgment

- Conflict Management, Cultural and situational awareness

- Organizational Process Assets

Stakeholder Mapping Techniques, e.g., Power/Interest Matrix, Salience Model

Tip

If you are subscribing to the *PMBOK® Guide* 7th edition, note the difference in terminology from ITTOs to Models, Methods, and Artifacts.

It is natural to want to control each step in the stakeholder life cycle. Spending time capturing details in a Stakeholder Register, mapping and analyzing stakeholders, and crafting a thoughtful communications plan only to find out one of your key stakeholders changed their outlook on the project is frustrating. It can feel like the work you did in the Identify and Plan stages was a waste. Though it may be upsetting to see a person devolve from Leading to Resistant in an Awareness/Attitude matrix, it is the nature of Stakeholder Engagement and should be expected by the project manager.

Tip

If the project uses stage gates, these are built-in opportunities to review lessons learned and investigate root causes if an event is significant.

Successful project managers have resilience and can rapidly reflect and move forward. They have a keen ability to see this change as a data point that is captured in the Lessons Learned Register rather than wallow or over-analyze why this happened.

Lessons Learned Register

Hindsight is 20/20 - in life and project management. Thankfully, project managers have the Lessons Learned Register to record information related to stakeholder engagement, e.g., challenges, successful approaches and messages, and suggestions to overcome problems in the future. At the closing of the current project, the Lessons Learned Register is added to the Lessons Learned Repository - an artifact that contains Registers from past projects to help inform future initiatives. The Lessons Learned Register is a productive approach to "not making the same mistake twice" and repeating effective strategies. Throughout a project, anyone on the team can identify an occurrence to include in the Lessons Learned Register. This is particularly helpful if there is a lengthy list of stakeholders to monitor and the responsibilities of engaging with certain groups or individuals are shared. Depending on how the project is tailored, the team may openly discuss lessons learned at milestones, stage gates, or end of sprints. Regardless of the frequency or designated junctures, the Lessons Learned Register is important for monitoring and managing stakeholders.

Issue Log

Ignorance is not bliss when it comes to managing issues related to project stakeholders. The best approach is to encourage people to share issues so the project manager can address each challenge and seek resolution. The Issue Log, shown in Table 7.2, is efficiently recorded in a table that can be similar in format to the Stakeholder Register. When the term issue log is used, it's reasonable to assume this means a technical log or a ticket system. In the context of Stakeholder Engagement, the Issue Log is an artifact used to aggregate issues that affect people, e.g., team dynamics, expectation misalignment, deliverable performance, and conflict. It's crucial that the project manager collect and manage each of the issues in the Log effectively to help ensure the project continues to progress as planned and stakeholders are engaged and aligned with goals.

Table 7.2   **Issue Log Example**

Issue	Issue Type	Concern From	Issue Details	Proposed Alternative	Issue Assigned To	Days to Resolve Date of the initial log to resolution addressed)
It was impossible to find where I needed to go on the website!	UX	Norma	I tried to use the search function, but no luck. Then, I tried to use the menu navigation and was unsuccessful. How do I find the mission and values section of the site?	Optimize the search function so it serves better results using more keywords.	Jim	3

The Issue Log documents the issue, outlines a potential resolution, and assigns a team member to address the issue. The Log should be specific, including the details of the concern, the name of the person who submitted it, the priority level, the suggested resolution, and who is responsible for closing the loop.

A skilled project manager will use the Issue Log artifact as a way to spot trends, see which stakeholders' expectations are not met, and ensure each issue is promptly addressed. Using the Issue Log to proactively review and add to this artifact helps keep stakeholders positively engaged and minimizes the chances that issues will balloon and spiral out of control.

Accounting for project sponsor expectations

On the subject of expectations, the project sponsor is just a

stakeholder so try to understand as much about them as you can - their style of communication, expectations about involvement, relationships with project team members, and their past behaviors on projects. Conversations with project sponsors - who are often in positions of authority and influence can be difficult. This is especially the case when the project sponsor defaults to blame when there are any challenges with stakeholders. It is not uncommon to have bumps in the road. How you anticipate, react, and mitigate issues is what will help your project get back on track as quickly as possible. For example, if you know your project sponsor is new to this role, try to take the time to educate them on the purpose of artifacts, e.g., Lessons Learned Register, Issue Log, and the Stakeholder Register. This helps you have a starting place when the Sponsor's urgent concerns become yours. Without these expectation level-setting early and often, sponsor questions can send the project manager whirling. You shold also expect that your project sponsor may be uninterested in learning about project management documents and terminology.

Now what? Do your best to stay organized so if issues arise, you are able to manage stakeholder concerns rather than frantically compile documents and look for how something got offtrack. Diagnosing stakeholder issues mid-project is time consuming and you risk getting distracted from advancing the project. In the case of the project sponsor, they are accountable for the success of the project so one approach is to attentively hear their concerns and ask them to prioritize what should be addressed to ensure the project isn't stalled. Remember, the project sponsor selects the project manager, not the other way around. The Sponsor, like all stakeholders, needs to be monitored and their expectations need to be taken into account. Once the Stakeholder Engagement Plan is in place, it is at regular intervals that the effectiveness of the plan is reviewed.

7.2 Methods to Manage and Monitor

In previous sections, you learned about the Lessons Learned Register and Issue Log, which are two useful artifacts as the project manager, and project team, seek to effectively monitor and manage the Stakeholder Engagement Plan. Let's review how to leverage these items to keep the project on track for success.

When applying the tools and artifacts in your arsenal, frame your thinking toward engagement rather than managing. No one wants to feel managed or monitored so finessing your approach is critical. Put another way, a project manager manages engagement with stakeholders through:

- Expert judgment

- Communication (informal and formal)

- Interpersonal and team skills

- Interviews

The project manager monitors the performance of the Stakeholder Engagement Plan through:

- Data analysis and visualization

- Decision making

- Communication (informal and formal)

- Interpersonal and team skills

- Meetings

Make sure to determine set reflection periods throughout the project - whether these are at milestones, at the end of sprints, or are structured based on frequency, e.g., monthly. Regardless of when or how the reviews are planned, the project manager should revisit the SEP as needed, especially when a significant event like a new project stakeholder occurs. Remember to remain people-centric and make sure the SEP enables you to have quality interactions. The SEP should also serve as a tool to measure the effectiveness of your engagement by indicating whether the right people are moving in the right direction. Recall the various stakeholder mapping and analysis tools and techniques from Chapter 3. The Stakeholder Register, Table 7.3, is one way to track which stakeholders are moving toward their Desired Engagement. At the onset of the project, the Current Engagement was assessed so now you have the opportunity to continue updating this column – hopefully nudging each stakeholder toward their Desired Engagement.

Table 7.3   **Stakeholder Register with the Current and Desired Engagement**

Name	Responsibility	Type (primary or secondary)	Power/ Interest (HH, HM, HL, MM, MH, ML, LH, LM, LL)	Sentiment (Positive, Negative, Neutral)	Current Engagement (unaware, resistant, neutral, supportive, leading)	Desired Engagement (unaware, resistant, neutral, supportive, leading)
John B.	Product Owner, Resource advocate	P	HH	P	Aware/ neutral	Aware/ leading
Michelle M.	Provide product supplies, manage supply chain	S	HL	P	Unaware	Aware/ neutral
Omar C.	Public Affairs	P	HM	Neu	Aware/ resistant	Aware/ supportive
Petra L.	Primary product user	P	LH	P	Aware/ supportive	Aware/ leading

Additionally, the Awareness/Attitude Matrix is a powerful visualization technique to help the project manager measure the effectiveness of their engagement with stakeholders. Similar to the Stakeholder Register in Table 7.3, if the Awareness/Attitude Matrix was created in an earlier stage of the project, the project manager can re-map the stakeholders to assess their current state. An example of this is in Figure 7.2.

| Figure 7.2 | Awareness/Attitude Matrix with current and desired state |

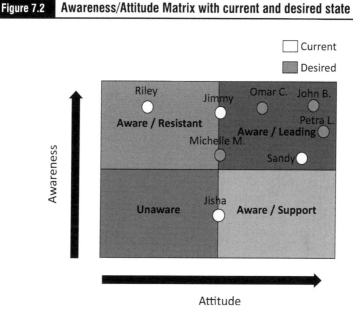

7.3 Working with Difficult Stakeholders

Working with stakeholders is already a moving goal post as you've learned throughout the book. Though there are seemingly endless scenarios where a project manager could label a stakeholder as "difficult," leading with empathy, practicing active listening, and seeking to manage expectations upfront should help temper the frustration that builds from working with difficult stakeholders. The idea is to "work" with difficult stakeholders to achieve a project goal. Even if you find that this is not a shared goal, if this person is on the project team, you can level-set expectations through the discussion of guiding principles at the project kickoff. This is helpful to include in the Project Charter as a way to reference how the team believes it should operate for this project so if a stakeholder behaves to the contrary, you can mention the touchstone document. Additionally, the Stakeholder Register, various mapping techniques, and SEP are at your fingertips to help you engage difficult stakeholders in a way that works for their personality and level of power/interest.

Regardless of the artifacts and soft skills you may employ, sometimes people can be a challenge. However, keep in mind that you do have options and should also continue to sharpen your skills in negotiation and conflict resolution to help you navigate challenging project stakeholders. Figures 7.3, 7.4, and 7.5 are situations you may encounter. By no means are these three types of stakeholders the only "difficult" ones you will encounter along your journey as a project manager. So, how can you see these people coming so you can either diffuse an otherwise heated conversation, swap them for a different project stakeholder, or help manage their expectations early and often? There are some questions to ask yourself as you engage diverse, and dynamic stakeholders throughout your career.

- How did the stakeholder become part of the project? Were they assigned? Did they raise their hand out of interest?

- How much authority or power does the stakeholder have in the organization (not just the project)?

- Does the stakeholder have a reputation for being an engaged or disengaged team member?

- Does the stakeholder have the bandwidth to be an active member of the project?

- What are your assessments of stakeholder attitudes toward the project, you as the project manager, and the project sponsor?

Expect the unexpected. And, do your best to anticipate people's behavior and update key artifacts, e.g., Stakeholder Register and SEP, based on the information you gather during interviews, meetings, and mapping exercises.

Figure 7.3 **The No Boundaries Stakeholder**

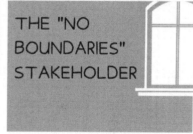

Figure 7.4   The Parachute Stakeholder

Figure 7.5   The Zombie Stakeholder

Case Study

By now, you have hopefully accepted the reality that a project manager must possess soft skills to accompany their technical prowess. The Manage and Monitor steps are the true test of this well-rounded competency so let's examine two project managers to determine where they are successful and where they open themselves up to increased risk. The instructor may ask the class to respond to both Tomás and Ava's situations or divide the class into two groups - assigning students to either Tomás or Ava.

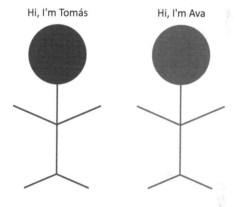

Hi, I'm Tomás   Hi, I'm Ava

Tomás is a newly minted project management professional (PMP) who just accepted the role of a senior project manager for the Office of Strategic Planning at Tiger Byte Hardware Solutions. Before this job, he worked as a product engineer at an oil and gas company where he oversaw a team of highly analytical and process-oriented individuals. He was recognized for three consecutive years for his company employee engagement scores. Tomás served in the military and is married with three children. He shines when there are rules and structure.

Discussion:

1. Tomás conducted the first iteration of the Stakeholder Register alongside the project sponsor. He feels confident he's identified all the legitimate stakeholders for this project and analyzed their power/interest at the onset of the project. Immediately following the first project milestone, a company Senior Director approached Tomás saying he should have been included.

> **What is the next step Tomás might consider now that he has this new information?**

2. Tomás is the project manager for the company's website redesign. During the soft launch, Tomás asked that people share any concerns by emailing him. As a result, he received hundreds of issues.

> **How might Tomás begin to untangle, prioritize, and update his Stakeholder Engagement Plan accordingly?**

3. Tomás is faced with a predicament for an enterprise-wide project he's leading. The project started "by the book," with the project sponsor attending the team's kickoff and reinforcing the charge outlined in the Project Charter. The Sponsor, Abel, conveyed that the budget was the most important aspect of the project, so the team should not only stay within budget, they should do whatever it takes to negotiate the best price with project vendors. The team proceeded with this directive.

Fast forward to the Planning phase and the team needed vendors for two aspects of the project - design and printing. Several key stakeholders made suggestions using expert judgment and a Lessons Learned Repository for vendor references. These key stakeholders felt confident in the potential vendor list and wanted to move forward with interviews and a proposal. Despite the trusted vendor recommendations, the project team opted to start from scratch issuing a request for proposal. They made this decision because of the expectation of the project sponsor to ensure the best price. This lengthy process and subsequent negotiations delayed the project - resulting in missed deadlines and rushed deliverables. Stakeholders were now upset about the condensed timelines to complete tasks and felt the in-depth vendor negotiations were unnecessary.

> **How might Tomás manage conflicting key stakeholder and project sponsor expectations?**

Ava has been at Tiger Byte Hardware Solutions for 8 years, working her way up from an assistant project manager in the regional division to a project manager at the national level. Ava is bilingual so she has had the opportunity to participate in projects working with suppliers in Latin America. Tiger Byte is poised to expand its customer base into Central America and Ava is eager to lead the business development initiative to assess the viability of this proposition. Ava's career has always been in project management. However, her college degree was in sociology and psychology. She is single and focused on her career. Ava recently took a personality assessment at Tiger Byte, which revealed her top strengths to be: Futuristic, Strategic, Activator, Goal-Oriented, and Self-Assurance.

1. Ava is angling to lead the business development initiative to evaluate expansion into Central America. She just found out that the current project she's running has many of the same stakeholders.

How might this adjust her Stakeholder Engagement plan strategies?

---

2. Ava has a robust Stakeholder Register with special attention to the expectations of high power / high interest stakeholders. The problem, however, is there are 30 people listed in the Register, 60 percent of whom are high power/high interest. She recently discovered there was a growing resistance among several key stakeholders because they felt they "haven't been appropriately engaged."

How might Ava address this and update the Stakeholder Engagement Plan accordingly?

Tomás and Ava were presented with situations that are familiar to project managers. Documenting any actions taken, suggested alternatives, issues raised, and lessons learned is essential. Some guidelines to effectively manage stakeholder engagement are:

- Seek to resolve conflict head-on and with urgency

- Keep asking Why, e.g., why does the stakeholder have this expectation or perspective? How could this impact their behavior on the projective?

- Connect the dots to determine if seemingly unrelated issues are part of a larger narrative.

- Keep trying. Just because a key stakeholder says they prefer emails doesn't preclude you from trying alternative methods of communication or email isn't engaging the person.

- Continue refining the SEP, updating the Stakeholder Register as needed, and finessing communications based on people's reactions to medium and messages.

Quiz

1. **The Lessons Learned Repository is _____**

    a. an artifact that contains Registers from past projects to help inform future initiatives.

    b. a document where team members confess mistakes.

    c. an artifact that only contains lessons learned from the current project.

    d. None of the above

2. **A project manager can manage engagement with stakeholders through one of the following?**

    a. Expert judgment

    b. Communication skills

    c. Both a and b

    d. Issuing directives

3. **A project manager manages engagement with stakeholders through all of the following EXCEPT _____**

    a. interpersonal and team skills

    b. ground rules

    c. meetings

    d. None of the above

4. **The Monitor process is part of which project phase?**

   a. Closing

   b. Planning

   c. Executing

   d. Monitoring and Controlling

5. **If the project manager uses a Lessons Learned Register, they do not need an Issue Log.**

   a. True

   b. False

6. **_____ is NOT a guideline to effectively manage stakeholder engagement.**

   a. Stick to the SEP without deviating

   b. Seek to resolve conflict head-on and with urgency

   c. Keep asking Why

   d. Connect the dots to determine if seemingly unrelated issues are part of a larger narrative.

7. **Which guideline is effective to manage stakeholder engagement?**

   a. Continue refining the SEP, updating the Stakeholder Register as needed, and finessing communications based on people's reactions to medium and messages.

   b. Keep trying. Just because a key stakeholder says they prefer emails doesn't preclude you from trying alternative methods of communication or email isn't engaging the person.

   c. Seek to resolve conflict head-on and with urgency

   d. All of the above

8. **An Issue Log is an artifact used to aggregate issues that affect people.**

   a. True

   b. False

9. **An Issue Log might include which of the following details?**

   a. Type of issue

   b. When the issue was resolved and by whom

   c. Date of issue submission

   d. All of the above

10. The artifact that captures lessons learned for the current project is called_____

   a. Lessons Learned Registry

   b. Lessons Learned Register

   c. Lessons Learned Repository

   d. None of the above

Answers	1 – a	2 – c	3 – d	4 – d	5 – b
	6 – a	7 – d	8 – e	9 – d	10 – b

Chapter Summary

◆ In the Stakeholder Engagement life cycle, each preceding step is a building block.

◆ In the Manage and Monitor steps, the project manager will engage, monitor, and re-engage stakeholders according to the Stakeholder Engagement Plan.

◆ When applying the tools and artifacts in your arsenal, frame the thinking toward engagement rather than managing.

◆ Successful project managers have resilience and are able to rapidly reflect and move forward.

◆ The Issue Log documents the challenge, outlines a potential resolution, and assigns a team member to address the issue. The Log should be specific, including the details of the concern, the name of the person who submitted it, the priority level, the suggested resolution, and who is responsible for closing the loop.

◆ Working with difficult stakeholders is tough, but project managers have tools and approaches they can reference to help navigate through these challenges.

◆ The Manage and Monitor processes are the 3rd and 4th steps in the Stakeholder life cycle.

Made in the USA
Middletown, DE
09 October 2024

62276211R00128